The Grateful
Gadsby

To The Patron's
of The Lois Wagner
Memorial Library.

Bill Gadsby
4

The Grateful Gadsby

How one of the NHL's greatest
defenseman found a balance between the wonder
of life and the violence of his sport

By Bill Gadsby
as told to Kevin Allen

Foreward by Mr. & Mrs. Hockey ®
Gordie and Colleen Howe

Published by Immortal Investments Publishing
35122 W. Michigan Avenue
Wayne, Michigan 48184
1 800 475-2066
www.Bill Gadsby.com
www.Immortal Investments.com

Publisher's Cataloging-in-Publication
(Provided by Quality Books, Inc.)

Gadsby, Bill.
    The grateful Gadsby : hockey, hardships & happiness /
by Bill Gadsby as told to Kevin Allen ; foreword by
Colleen and Gordie Howe. -- 1st ed.
    p. cm.
    "How one of the NHL's greatest defensemen found a
balance between the wonder of life and the violence of
his sport."
    LCCN 2002115731
    ISBN 0-9723637-0-X

    1. Gadsby, Bill. 2. Hockey players--United States--
Biography. 3. Hockey coaches--United States--Biography.
4. National Hockey League--History.   I. Allen, Kevin,
1956- II. Title.

GV848.5.G347A3 2003   796.962'092
                        QBI33-999

I dedicate this book to my personal
All Star team, my family, what a line up !

Acknowledgments

I thank Gord and Colleen Howe for urging me to tell my story. To Kevin Allen for his talent in writing this book. To Del, Marty and Mike Reddy for their work in putting it all together and to my family, friends and fans, who without them there would not be a grateful Gadsby. Above all I thank the Lord!

Photo Credits

Cover picture courtesy of Dwayne Labakas.
Family portraits courtesy of Breckenridge Studios, owner Donna L. Williams.
Clarence the Lion courtesy of Florida's Homosassa Springs.
Photos scanned by Story Technologies LLC David M. Story and James D. Zech.

Foreword

When our son Marty was a youngster he once asked us for a couple of dollars and we just assumed he wanted to guzzle down a soda or buy a candy bar. But he wanted the money to purchase Bill Gadsby one of his favorite cigars. What makes that story more interesting is that we were with the Detroit Red Wings at that point, and Bill was playing with the rival New York Rangers.

Bill thought we told Marty to do that but it was strictly his idea. That's how much respect he had for Bill. He didn't care that Bill was wearing a Rangers' sweater. That's the kind of impact Bill Gadsby has on people.

We've been friends with Bill and Edna for 50 years, and we've never met two finer people. When hockey players become friends, they never know whether their wives will share the same bond. The four of us instantly became best friends from our first meeting. What's funny is that in the Original Six era players don't fraternize with players from an opposing team. And yet the Gadsbys and Howes became friends long before we played together on the Red Wings. Bill was with the New York Rangers when we got together the first time on a Saskatchewan lake.

Bill and Edna are more family than friends. We view their children as our nieces, and our children consider them as an aunt and uncle. In our playing days, the Gadsbys and Howes spent some holidays together. We even vacationed together.

When Marty was a real young player we told him to pattern himself after an NHL player, and right away he picked Bill. What can be said about Bill is everyone loved him as a person and they hated to play against him.

At game time, Bill was a warrior. You won't find a more competitive athlete. He was skilled, tough, fearless. He could play mean in the name of winning. But he was an honest player. He hit you square up. He hit you fairly, and when the game was over he was as gentlemanly of a soul as you would ever meet. The Gadsbys were the kind of people you hoped all of your neighbors would be.

One year for Bill and Edna's anniversary we surprised them with a trip to Hawaii. We wouldn't even tell them where they were going until we were in California. That was great fun. This relationship worked well because the guys liked to pal around together playing golf and fishing and the women were very close. We had our most fun when the four of us were together, or when the families were merged.

We used to drop hints with the Red Wings that they should try to acquire Bill in a trade. The problem was that the Rangers wouldn't cooperate. They liked Bill too much. We thought the Red Wings finally had landed Bill in 1960, and then Red Kelley wouldn't report to New York and the deal was canceled. Finally the Red Wings got Bill in 1961.

We were so thankful when we heard that the Gadsbys were coming to Detroit. We started looking for places for them to live the minute we heard.

The Red Wings gave up Les Hunt in the deal. He should feel pretty good about that trade because truthfully he was traded for two Hall of Fame people – Bill and Edna Gadsby.

Mr. & Mrs. Hockey ®
Gordie and Colleen Howe

Bill Gadsby

Player Profile

- Turned Pro (18 years old) Youngest defenseman in NHL.
- 20 years-NHL (1946-1966) 2nd player in history to do so.
- 7 All Star Selections: Only defenseman in history to play in. 3 different All Star games with 3 different teams.
- Retired as all time point leader for a defenseman.
- Played 1248 Season Games- Retired as all time defensive leader for games played and penalty minutes garnered.
- Played 67 Playoff Games.
- Runner-up 3 Times Norris Trophy.
- Assist Record for NHL Defenseman in (1959).
- First Defenseman in N.H.L. to Score 500 career Pts. (1962)
- Career Record: 130 Goals & 437 Assists.
- Voted in Top 100 N.H.L. Players of All Time (1998).

<u>1970 INDUCTION</u>
<u>NHL HALL OF FAME</u>

- Member of.... Red Wing Hall Of Fame.
  Michigan Sports Hall Of Fame.
  Alberta Sports Hall OF Fame.
- Chicago Blackhawks (8 Years)
- New York Rangers   (7 Years)
- Detroit Red Wings   (5 Years)

Chapter 1

My wife Edna has always felt as though she has been married to two different men. She was married to William Alexander Gadsby, rough and tumble Hall of Fame National Hockey League defenseman, who amassed 1,539 penalty minutes, most of them well deserved.

That's the same Bill Gadsby who nearly started a riot in Montreal one night because he climbed into the stands during a game in a futile attempt to exact revenge against Butch Bouchard.

That's the same Gadsby who leveled Tim Horton on what some folks claim is one of the roughest body checks ever thrown at Maple Leaf Gardens. It's the same Gadsby who finished his NHL career with the memory of 640 stitches, 11 broken noses, many broken toes, a fractured fibula and a shoulder that was broken so badly that the bone still protrudes two inches higher than it should.

The other Bill Gadsby, the one that Edna knows better than anyone, is the man who started calling her sweetheart a week after he walked her home for the first time. It's the same man who sent her about 150 letters from the day he joined the NHL in 1946 until the day he married her in 1952.

It's the same man who wrote a letter to his first-born, Brenda, when she was only four months old advising her to behave for her mother and wishing her the best of luck in trying to eat rather than wear all of her carrots.

Those who have watched me putter around my flower garden or identify the birds who frequent my yard say I'm simply too polite to have been the same man who once shoved a NHL referee or speared a policeman in my effort to chase down an opposing player. Those who know me as a church usher can't believe that when I retired from the NHL in 1966 after 20 years of service, I was the leagues all-time penalty minute leader. Honestly, I never felt as if there was a contradiction in how I conducted myself on the ice and off the ice.

Before my father, Bill Sr., sent me off to play in the NHL, he offered me one piece of advice that I've always tried to follow; never bring the game home with you. Finally, he made one request that I've also tried to honor. "Bill, I've given you a name with a good reputation," my Dad said. "I want you to keep that good reputation." To me, what that meant was setting high standards for myself on and off the ice. My father was a soccer player, and by all accounts, he was a rough soccer player. I knew him as a man who won prizes for growing flowers and liked to putter in his garden.

As an athlete, I felt as if I owed my coach, my teammates and the fans my best every night. As an athlete, I felt I had to stand up for my teammates and myself. As an athlete, I felt I couldn't cheat the talent I had been blessed with.

That was the code I lived by as a player, and it really wasn't much different than the code I lived by as a husband and father. As a husband, I believed as if I had to do whatever I could to make sure Edna was comfortable and appreciated. As a father, I felt as if I had to do all I could to make sure my four daughters had a happy childhood and were prepared for adult life. Sometimes that meant taking them to see the Christmas tree every year at Rockefeller Center in New York and sometimes it meant timing our trips home from New York and Detroit every year to make sure they didn't miss a day of a school.

To me, I wasn't two different people, as much as I was one man who believed he had to do the best he could every day as a husband, father and hockey player. That's how my parents raised me. I knew no other way. Whether I was blocking a shot or playing with my children, I remembered what my parents had taught me.

From the day I started in the National Hockey League in 1946-47 with the Chicago Blackhawks until the day I retired from the Detroit Red Wings in 1965-66, I felt as if I was in the midst of combat. Each game was a battle, a physical confrontation between athletes who felt like they had to prove they belonged in the NHL every day they were in it.

One night Bobby Hull hit me with a shot in the solar plexus that rendered me unconscious for several seconds. I played the next shift.

The reason I know how many stitches I had is that my dear wife, Edna, kept a log of how many times I was hurt, just like some spouses keep a list of birthdays and anniversary dates. That was just part of our life.

When some local insurance man started offering players stitch insurance I signed up immediately. Under terms of the $100 policy, I would receive $5 for every stitch I received that season. A few days after I bought the policy, Toronto Maple Leafs winger Hugh Bolton sent a rocket screaming toward the net. Just as he completed his follow-through, Bill Mosienko skated in front of me and I never saw the puck until it split open my lower lip with a cut that seemed to be as wide as the Grand Canyon. The final tally was 30 stitches. It was the ugliest gash of my career. My diet consisted of a tea and toast for about three weeks. I lost 11 pounds.

In the midst of all that misery I had to laugh at the poor agent who sold me that stitch insurance. In less than two weeks I had paid for the policy. I had gotten back all my money, plus a $50 profit. I think they stopped offering that policy not long after that.

When I think back on my playing days, Edna was simply an angel during all of my injuries. Talk about taking your husband for better or worse, if my stitches were ready to be removed and the doctor was unavailable, Edna would get out a small pair of scissors and some tweezers and remove them herself. If that isn't love, what is?

In reviewing my career, I'm proud that I left the NHL as the highest scoring defenseman in NHL history. I'm more proud of the fact that Gordie Howe and I were the first players to play 1,000 games. I feel quite good that I left the game with a reputation of a man who played through many injuries. When the Red Wings acquired me at age 34 in 1961, Boston Bruins' great Eddie Shore said of the deal; "He will play three to five more years. He is virtually indestructible." That kind of praise means plenty to me because it meant that I never cheated on my effort.

In the days of Original Six hockey, to play through injury, pain and discomfort was expected as much as it was admired. The tradition passed down from generation to generation. When I came up with the Blackhawks in 1946-47, I watched teammate John Mariucci slather liniment oil over his body to minimally reduce the pain he would endure just to play. He played often on nights when he could barely walk into the dressing room. He was the toughest man I ever met. Mariucci was as revered in our dressing room as any player on the team, including Max and Doug Bentley, and Bill Mosienko. The Bentleys, in particular, thought the world of Mariucci because he looked after them like they were his brothers. If you attempted to harm any player on that line, Mariucci would be serving as your jury, judge and executioner.

In the Original Six days, we policed ourselves, and for the most part did a very good job of it. With only six teams in the league, you played each team 14 times during the regular season. If someone did something you didn't like in one game, you might be playing him the next night in your arena or the following weekend. We played a lot of home and home series against each other. The intensity of the rivalry in those years is difficult to explain to those who didn't live in that world. Often we ended up on the same trains heading back to finish a home-and-home, and we would walk through a car not saying a word to players from the other team.

Forty years later those of us who played in the Original Six era can remember hits and plays like they happened yesterday. The funny thing is that when many of us get together these days we're just as likely to remember what occurred off the ice. This wasn't just a sport to us, it was our way of life.

When Edna and I reminisce about yesteryear we don't talk about how I made the All-Star team seven times; we talk about the circumstances that led gangster Al Capones brother Matty ending up as one of the babysitters for our daughter Brenda. We talk about how when I took Edna to a Chicago nightclub for the first time, the bandleader announced there were celebrities in the house and she started to crane her neck with the hope of seeing a movie star. We still laugh about how disappointed Edna was when she learned that the bandleader was just talking about the Chicago Blackhawks, the same fellows Edna saw four or five times a week. They were my teammates, my buddies. To Edna, they weren't stars.

Once during a golf game, a fellow said he had a trivia question and asked who was the only defenseman to be named an All-Star while playing with three different teams. I had no idea. The answer was Bill Gadsby. Those kinds of accomplishments just didn't register with me, and still don't.

I can't tell you how many points I had in what year, but I can tell you that legendary Detroit weatherman Sonny Elliot played Santa Claus at the Red Wings Christmas party. I remember that because my girls loved those parties.

When you read my story, you will learn that I had some traumatic events in my life, and yet as I look back all I can feel is that I was blessed for all of my life. I've celebrated my 50th wedding anniversary, and all of my daughters grew up to be healthy and wonderful adults. They married fine men, and raised good children.

I had a great NHL career, and even though I'm in my 70s I can still shoot in the 80s for a round of golf.

It's always puzzling to me when people ask if I felt cheated because I never won a Stanley Cup. Cheated? I feel humbled that I was allowed to have the good life I have enjoyed.

When people talk about Original Six Era hockey, they talk about how rough and mean the games could be. That was certainly true, but when I think of my life in that era I remember that I worked just as hard to find Farmers Wife baby formula for my oldest daughter Brenda than I did to keep the puck out of my net. Brenda was born in Edmonton in 1953, and our family pediatrician told Edna to start her on Farmers Wife formula. Considering how big Chicago was, it never occurred to Edna that she might not be able to find that particular brand. We were on the road in Montreal when Edna called exasperated to say that no one in Chicago carried Farmers Wife. No problem, I told Edna, I'm sure they sell that brand in Montreal. Sure enough, the local supermarket had it and I bought a whole case. There was no room in my suitcase for 24 large cans of formula, so I gave every one of my teammates a can or two to carry back. When you think of Original Six hockey, you might think about the night that I broke Tim Horton's jaw and leg with a single check. When Edna and I think about Original Six hockey we think of the Blackhawks getting off the train and one-by-one handing me Farmer's Wife Baby Formula. Sometimes the guys would forget, and would have to lug the can or cans to practice the next day. Any man can throw his body in front of a Rocket Richard slap shot, but it takes a really tough man to carry another mans baby formula down the street.

Chapter 2

About the time that the movie careers of Roy Rogers and Hopalong Cassidy were hitting full gallop in the mid-to late-1930's, yours truly was starting to ride with dreams of being a National Hockey League player.

The happenings on the big screen were important to me as a youngster growing up in Calgarys North Hill area because the bulbs of the Crescent Theater marquee on 17th Avenue and Center Street doubled as lights for the makeshift outdoor hockey rink where my skills were born.

In the summer, that parcel of land was a community garden where families worked together to plant tomatoes, squash, corn and a variety of other vegetables that would end up on our dinner plate. But the importance of the land to the neighborhood boys came in winter, after the first snowfall, when the Calgary fire department would hose it down to create a neighborhood hockey rink.

My father, William Sr., would borrow the neighbors hoses and hook them together to provide enough footage to reach the rink. He made it his job to make sure enough water got to the rink to keep the ice as firm as possible. In the spring, he would add his water bills together and divide the total by the number of families who used the outdoor rink. All of the neighbors paid their fair share. That was agreed upon in advance.

From the age of about seven until I began playing regularly on organized teams at age 13, I played on that rink about every minute that I wasn't at school. The wonder of the location was that we could play well into the night because the theater marquee would illuminate half the rink. As dusk descended upon Calgary, we simply moved the game down to the theater end of the ice. Everyone in the neighborhood knew that their kids would be home as soon as the marquee went dark; some time between 9 and 10 o'clock.

The only time we wouldn't be playing hockey was Cowboy Saturday, when we would be paying a dime for admission into the Crescent to watch Roy Rogers latest adventure with Trigger. To be truthful, on some Saturdays 10 cents was hard to come by and only one of us would actually pay for a ticket. It was his job to sneak down the aisle to the back door and crack it enough for all of us to squeeze in, one at a time.

In the darkness, we would scamper up one of the aisles like commandos trying to avoid enemy sentries. As soon as we found a vacant row, we would dive in. One can imagine the surprise of those already in their seats to see the heads of several youngsters seemingly popping up out of nowhere.

After the picture show it would be back to the rink where you would play six or seven games before the Crescent flicked the marquee switch. When you are eight, nine, ten, eleven and twelve, you felt as if you could play hockey twenty-four hours a day. You were never tired. You probably wouldn't even have eaten if it were not for your mother calling you in for supper.

I never worried about anything in those days except playing hockey. My parents did all the worrying for me. Only after I married Edna and had four beautiful daughters of my own, did I realize how much my parents did for me as a youngster.

My father and mother, Elizabeth (called Liz by her friends) were both Great Britain natives who had come to Canada in search of a new life. They were hard working immigrants with a great appreciation for family values and living their life with great dignity and grace. My wife Edna still has a 54-year-old letter, in my fathers beautiful penmanship, thanking her for a cup and saucer she had brought my parents when they met for the first time in 1947.

In the letter, they wrote Edna saying they were looking forward to meeting her. They addressed it to Miss Anfindsen. When they sent her the thank you letter, it was addressed to Edna. That's the way my parents were.

My parents were survivors; a skill that was crucial to my mother and me when the Germans were trying to make us a World War II casualty in 1939. That is a story I will be telling later in this book.

Elizabeth Gadsby was a determined woman. She lived in her own home into her 90s, and she lived five days beyond her 100th birthday. She was a remarkable woman.

My father worked for more than 50 years in baggage delivery, first for the Canadian Pacific Railway and then as an independent agent. He rarely missed a day of work. Maybe he passed that on to his sons because my older brother worked 54 years for CPR, starting as a 15-year-old Red Cap and advancing all the way to becoming the Baggage Master. In those 54 years, he missed only one day of work. That's right, he missed one shift in 54 years.

In my twenty NHL seasons the only games I missed were the games that the team doctor ordered me not to play. To me, playing through broken toes and bruised ribs just came with the job.

Maybe I inherited my toughness from my father as well. Before I was born he was a top level soccer player, and I've talked to guys who played against him in Calgary who swear my father was a ruthless competitor.

Although his background was in soccer, he certainly loved hockey. He organized an industrial hockey league in Calgary. CPR would sponsor a team, as would the Calgary Fire Department and Police Department. Some other businesses would have teams. It was pretty good hockey. My dad would let me practice with those teams when I was seven, eight and ten years old. Sure I got banged around a little bit, but maybe that helped prepare me for what was ahead of me as a pro hockey player.

We didn't have much money, but my parents always figured out a way to get by. My father would bring home cracked sticks and we would repair them using scrap tin plating from Chesneys Hardware on 16th Avenue. Hockey players, particularly NHL players, like their skates to be one or two sizes smaller than their shoe size to assure a tight fit. But sometimes I would end up with skates three sizes too big and we would stuff the toes with newspaper. The Gadsbys always found a way to provide for their family.

My mother was twenty-two when Harold was born. She was thirty-eight when I was born. She would always tell me, you were a mistake, but you were a wonderful mistake.

To be honest, I don't really know whether my parents actually believed I would end up in the National Hockey League. My father understood that I was a talented player, but he also told me that if I didn't have a professional career by the time I was 20 he could get me a job at CPR like Harold had.

As confident as I was in my hockey playing ability, there were a bushel of reasons for my parents to remind me to be practical. Harold was also a talented hockey player. He was probably talented enough to have played in the NHL but a serious knee injury ended his career prematurely. And let's not forget that the NHL only had six teams back then, and there were only about 30 NHL jobs for defensemen. If you think in those terms, my odds probably didn't seem too good to my parents.

However they certainly supported my sports career even to the point of allowing me, at age seventeen in 1944, to move to Edmonton to play junior hockey. They also allowed me to try out with the American Hockey Leagues Cleveland Barons when I was sixteen. Cleveland's scout, Pete Egan, brother of Boston Bruins player Pat Egan, had spotted me playing in Calgary. He had invited me to attend a tryout camp first in Windsor, Ontario. My parents weren't convinced it was the best thing for me to travel alone across the country. But they decided to allow me to go.

Although the Barons weren't in the NHL, they were an important team in that era of hockey. Former

NHL standout Bun Cook was the coach when I attended the Barons training camp. In the 1940s, he won five AHL championships coaching that team. Some very talented players wore the Barons jersey. Les Cunningham, who had earlier played with the Chicago Blackhawks in 1939-40, was a fixture on that team.

The Cleveland organization treated players well enough that it was almost as if they were in the NHL. The year after I got my tryout, Johnny Bower came to the Barons and they basically had to force him to go the NHL. He had a good job in Cleveland, and just didn't want to leave the team. When I went there for my tryout the team had several players from Western Canada, including Tommy Burlington, and brothers Bob and
Bill Carse, who were all from Edmonton. Burlington played in the AHL with only one eye.

What I remember most about Cleveland days was my physical appearance on the day I left.

As a youngster I didn't confine my sports participation just to the hockey rink; I played plenty of baseball and football. The junior football in Calgary was quite good in the 1940s with each section of the city boasting a strong team. We would play in the same stadium that the Canadian Football Leagues Calgary Stampeders played. My team was the North Hill Blizzard, and in 1944 we played in the city championship game. That game was scheduled for the day before I was to board the train for Windsor.

At 185 pounds, I was one of the biggest players on the North Hill squad. I played pulling tackle, and I played on both sides of the ball. As you can imagine, I liked the physical contact. I liked to be in the middle of the play. We wore leather helmets in those days and no

protective bar in front. Late in the championship I was
on the ground after making a tackle and someone fell on
top of me and drove my nose into the ground. At that
point, I didn't know all that much about broken noses.
But it was pretty clear from the awful sound and the
pain, that it was fractured. Later that day a doctor had
to snap the nose back in place. If there was talk about
me not making that trip to Windsor for my Barons'
tryout, I certainly don't remember it. My parents
understood what it meant for me to try out for a pro
team. The doctor affixed a bandage to my nose and
used two pieces of tape to hold it in place. With the
swelling and purplish tint, my face was monstrous to
behold.

      Imagine what the Barons thought when I showed
up looking like I had lost a bar fight. But it didn't
effect my playing ability. I made the cut at the Barons
camp in Windsor. I was one of the youngest players
chosen to practice with the club in Cleveland.
It's funny what you remember about an experience, and
what you forget. Can't remember much at all about the
hockey that was played during my time at the Barons
camp, but I remember all of the ushers at the Cleveland
arena wore sharp dark blazers with snazzy bright red
ties. I thought they looked quite spiffy.

      Although the Barons didn't offer me a contract,
just the experience gave me added motivation. They
talked about wanting to keep an eye on me, but
truthfully I was already thinking about the NHL.

      My decision to play for the Edmonton
Canadians certainly was the best decision I ever made.
As a player in Edmonton, I had two great seasons with
the Canadians. I was the leagues most valuable player
in my final year there and showed enough spark as a

rushing defenseman to have the Chicago Blackhawks eager to sign me.

As a young man in Edmonton, I met the girl who has been my sweetheart for more than half a century. Her name was Edna Anfindsen, a petite, beautiful 17-year-old girl who had every right to be as choosy as she pleased. She was bright, charming and full of life. We met at the Cozy Corner, a combination coffee/ice cream shop, on the corner of 112th Avenue and 65th Street.

Edna's friend, Charlie Holloway, brought Vince Bannon and I into the shop to get a Coca Cola on our way to get set-up for a part-time job at the sheet metal factory. If you came from another city to play hockey in Edmonton, it was customary for the team to find you a job.

Not long before we came to the Cozy Corner, all the players had received their sharp white and red team jackets.

Edna was only in the Cozy Corner that afternoon because she was babysitting the owners granddaughter. She has told the story many times about how she was sitting at the counter and noticing how handsome we looked coming into that shop dressed in our new jackets. She has always said that Bannon looked like a young Tyrone Power.

Maybe it was my good fortune that Bannon was injured in practice that day because he was unable to attend a social gathering at an Edmonton families home that included Edna among the guests. When the party broke up, I asked Edna if I could walk with her the three or four blocks to her home. We immediately started dating. It's really hard to call it dating because really what we did most often was that I would give

Edna a ticket to one of the Edmonton Canadian games and then I would walk her home afterward. She only lived two blocks from the Edmonton Gardens, where we played.

Even if I hadn't fallen in love with Edna, the post-game food she prepared for me probably would have been enough to keep me returning.

Lars and Bertha Anfindsen were Norwegians who immigrated to Saskatchewan in 1926, not long after losing their oldest daughter to illness. They moved to Edmonton when Edna was ten and they lived very modestly in a small home. Lars was a skilled hunter, and one of his walks through the wheat fields outside of Edmonton was like a trip to the grocery store. He knew all of the farmers, and he had permission to hunt all over the area. He would come back every weekend with enough pheasant, ducks, geese and partridge to feed his family for weeks at a time.

Throughout my NHL career, I saw players who simply had a keen instinct for hockey; they knew what to do and where to be at all times.

That's the way Lars was with hunting; through the years he would take to his favorite hunting spots and the sky would always be black with geese and ducks. He just knew where the prey was going to be.

There was no money for a freezer, so after the birds were cleaned Bertha would cook them immediately and can them.

The Anfindsens always went to bed early, and the house would be quiet when Edna would bring me home after my game. She would ask her mother if it was okay to feed me and she was always told to go to the basement and get one of the jars. What that meant was that I was about to have a meal that you would pay top dollar for in a nice restaurant.

The basement of the Anfindsen home had rows of jarred birds, not to mention home-canned peaches and other fruits. Edna would add some milk and flour to the mix on the stove, and then serve it on toast. What a feast it was.

Can you imagine what my parents must have thought when I wrote about having a girl who fed me pheasant and partridge for my post-game meal?

The Anfindsens were delightful people, but Lars was a strict father. After I would be there about an hour, he would yell from the bedroom, "it's time to go home Bill," and I would do just that.

It didn't take long for Edna to realize that I didn't have the same manners on the ice as I did in her home. She became accustomed to the idea that I often was going to be in the middle of rough play. But it was never easy for her.

In my second season with the Edmonton Canadians, on a night when I was to be honored as the leagues most valuable player, I went sliding into the opposing netminder and my skate caught under his belly pad. The wound I gave him needed 15 stitches to close. Even though it was an accident, fans started booing me. Edna was sitting in the stands when this was all going on. She has always been sympathetic to the families of athletes who get booed because she knew what it was like to hear fans raining down insults and catcalls on me.

There was no question my relationship with Edna was serious from the beginning. But we were both so young that we didn't think all that much about the future.

I was playing well enough in Edmonton that a

pro career seemed likely. It was clear in my second year that the Chicago Blackhawks viewed me as having plenty of promise. Edna told me later that she presumed that I would go off to the big city of Chicago and meet some American gal and she would be forgotten. That's not the way I viewed the situation, but my focus was clearly on hockey.

When it was time to negotiate my first professional contract no one had ever heard of the concept of a player agent. But in 1946 my Edmonton junior coach Earl Robertson probably helped in my dealings with the Chicago Blackhawks as well any modern agent could have.

Probably the Blackhawks thought I would sign any contract they put in front of me. Maybe I would have accepted their first offer if Robertson, a former NHL player, hadn't been advising me.

In those days, there was no player draft. NHL teams sponsored clubs, and if you ended up on one of their junior teams your rights belonged to that team.

With only six NHL teams and each team only carrying 16 players, there weren't many NHL jobs to be had.

Team officials knew that every Canadian teen-age boy dreamed of playing in the NHL, and when it came time to sign a player they showed you the contract and let you know they were doing you a favor by allowing you to play. It wasn't hard to convince a teen-age player that if he didn't take the deal that was offered, it would simply be given to another player in another Canadian town who would be thrilled to have the money you were rejecting.

Even before Chicago president and general manager Bill Tobin showed up in Edmonton for the contract meeting, it had been made clear to me that the Blackhawks were interested in signing me. The Blackhawks sponsored several teams, and word had gotten around that they were interested in taking goaltender Emile Francis, left wing Bert Olmstead and center Metro Prystai of the Moose Jaw Canucks. It certainly had helped my bargaining power that they had watched me play my best hockey at the 1946 Memorial Cup. I had 12 goals in 14 games.

When Robertson heard I was to meet with Bill Tobin and Blackhawks Chief scout Tiny Thompson at the MacDonald Hotel , he drew up a plan as if he was preparing to coach in a playoff game. He told me he would get a room at the McDonald, and when the Blackhawks presented the contract offer I was to make up some excuse about needing to call my father. What he really wanted me to do was to bring the offer to him so he could tell me what to do.

Robertson had plenty of credibility as far as I was concerned. He had played goaltender for the New York Americans and Detroit Red Wings. In fact, eight years before he had been called up from the minors to replace an injured Clint Smith and ended up winning a Stanley Cup championship with the Red Wings. Robertson was a good coach, and he seemed to have a real knack for understanding how the system worked.

As much as I trusted Robertson, I knew it wouldn't be easy for me to negotiate with Tobin and Thompson. Remember I'm 18 and these guys seemed like they had the power to make or break my career. Before Tobin gave me his offer, he told me he was offering me more than he usually gives new players. He said he was doing that because he really liked me as a player.

The offer was $5,000 per year plus a $1,500 signing bonus. I was impressed by the speech and impressed by the money. I was ready to sign. But dutifully I did what coach Robertson asked, I excused myself from Tobin and Thompson by saying something about wanting to call my parents. Instead, I went to Robertson's room.

"You can get more than that," Robertson said. "They want you bad. Tiny Thompson is bubbling about you. I know you have what it takes to play there. You can have a good career. Maybe you might have to go to the minors for a month or two, but you are close to being ready. You may as well get some money now."

If Robertson was trying to build up my confidence, it was working.

"You go up there and tell them you want $9,000 salary and $3,000 to sign," Robertson added.

The idea of asking for that much money exhilarated me and petrified me at the same time. Robertson obviously sensed that the idea of demanding more money terrified me. My thought was, "what if I tick them off and they don't want to sign me at all?"

"They will fall off their chairs," Robertson said, smiling. "But you do what I tell you."

When I told the Blackhawks brass what I wanted, they reacted as Robertson said they would. Thompson was so angry he stalked out of the room. Tobin was calmer, but no less miffed.

"There are guy's who have been in the league eight or nine years who aren't making $9,000," Tobin insisted.

My ego must have doubled in size between the time I left Robertson's room until the time I came back to talk to Tobin and Thompson because I didn't flinch when Tobin resisted.

"I don't care what everyone else is making," I said. "That's what I want to play, and I think it will pay off for you."

Tobin said he needed time to think about it, and I headed back to Robertson where I suggested that perhaps I should come down on my demands.

"Keep that price up. You can always come down, but you can't go up," he said. "If you get $7,000 you will be doing great. They think you are going to be a good player. They will give it to you."

When I came back Tobin had increased his offer by $500, and I told him I had to leave again. After I would visit with Robertson, I would drop my asking price by $500. This went on several times, enough times that Robertson had moved from the room to the bar. Finally we settled on $7,000 and a $3,000 signing bonus, but only after I had made one final visit to Robertson in the bar.

I didn't buy Robertson a drink for his services, but I should have. That $3,000 signing bonus seemed like $3 million to me. No need to sneak into the Crescent Theater anymore. I could afford the 10 cents for admission.

Chapter 3

If all National Hockey League rookies truly must have a baptism under fire, mine came the night John Mariucci and Black Jack Stewart fought as if they were gladiators locked in mortal combat.

The date was February 16, 1946, and I was a nineteen-year-old rookie with about twenty-five NHL games to my credit when Mariucci and Stewart gave me a lesson about the toughness required to survive in the NHL. It started innocently enough when Gordie Howe checked Doug Bentley into the boards, and his brother Max thought it came just a second after the whistle and he immediately went after Gordie. Then Sid Abel jumped into the fray to even the score. As was his custom, Mariucci made it his business to look after the Bentleys and he went in swinging. Seconds later, Stewart confronted Mariucci and both men had their fists pounding away like jackhammers against each others
face.

Few professional boxing matches have come close to matching the intensity of this bare-knuckle battle

between two of the roughest competitors ever to wear a
NHL sweater.

Estimates vary about how long they actually traded
punches, but my recollection was they stood toe-to-toe
and exchanged right hands for about three minutes.
Then after they were separated, they were led off to the
penalty box. As soon as the linesmen had skated away,
the punches began flying once again. The fight spilled
over in the corridors. As all of this was going on, I was
on the bench and I remember saying to no one in
particular, " Geez, do these guys fight like this all the
time?"

Everyone thought that was pretty funny. That
scrap certainly was the most famous hockey fight of that
era, and many believe it was one of the most ferocious
battles in the history of hockey.

When the fight was over, the penalty box always
seemed to be filled the rest of the night. The game was
2-2 with less than two minutes left when we came down
to a 3-on-3 situation on the ice. Here I was sitting
wide-eyed on the bench, trying to sort in my mind what
I had just witnessed when I hear Coach Johnny
Gotteselig ask the Bentleys, " Who do you want on the
ice with you?" "Give us the kid," Max says. When
Gottselig nodded for me to get on the ice, there was a
fair amount of pride dripping from me as a I jumped
over the boards. To be honest, I was confident in my
ability to play in the NHL once I got there. But the
Bentleys were among the most talented players in the
league, and when they asked for me to be the
defensemen out there with them, it made me feel as if
they saw potential in me.

With the clock winding down, Max sent a pass my
way inside the Detroit blue line and I buried it past

Harry Lumley with one second left on the clock to give us a 3-2 win. The shot beat Lumley cleanly. Lumleys jaw dropped when the puck zipped past him. He was no doubt stunned to be beaten by a rookie. " He was the most disgusted goalie I've ever seen," was my quote in the newspaper the next day.

If I had any doubts about my ability to play in the NHL, they were erased that night.

To Earl Robertson's credit, he knew what he was talking about when he said the Blackhawks wanted me badly. Blackhawks' President and GM Bill Tobin had told me that I would be in Kansas City in the United States Hockey League just to get a feel for pro hockey. Former Blackhawks player Elwin Doc Romnes was coach there, and they assumed I would pick up a few tips from him about playing at the next level. They made it clear that they planned to bring me up as soon as the opportunity presented itself. It was understood that defenseman Reg Hamiltons was on his last leg, and they seemed to have me penciled in as his replacement.

When Hamilton started getting worse just before Thanksgiving, I was called up. My minor league career had lasted twelve games and twenty-seven stitches.

As much as I may have learned from Doc Romnes in a short period, I may have learned more from Nick Knott, a forward with the Tulsa team. In my first professional game, playing against Tulsa, I went into the corner with Knott, gave him just a quick elbow, and came out with a cut on my forehead. Blood washed over my face like it was a waterfall. That taught me quickly that this wasn't junior hockey, and I had to be ready to protect myself at all times. What overwhelmed rookies in their first game at Chicago Stadium in the 1940s wasn't what they saw, but rather what they could hear, or maybe more accurately said, what they couldn't hear.

When I laid eyes on Chicago Stadium for the first time, it was empty and yet it still seemed like a hockey palace. The old barn, with a seating capacity of just over 20,000, looked spacious enough to hold the population of Calgary when it was empty. I was coming from playing in Edmonton where we would draw 4,000 people and that seemed like I was playing in front of the whole world. Those grand balconies made Chicago Stadium seem even more spacious than it was.

As awe-struck as you were at the sight of Chicago Arena, you were still unprepared how the building came to life when a game was being played. The noise in that building was almost deafening when the Blackhawks took the ice to play a National Hockey League game. The raucous nature of Chicago fans was enhanced by the sounds of a Barton organ that was built specifically for the acoustics for the arena. The pipes were built into the walls of the arena, and the balconies were designed to hang over the arena and the sound would just bounce back toward the playing surface. It was always said that when the organ was played at full volume, the noise level was the equivalent of twenty-five brass bands playing in an enclosed area. That wasn't an exaggeration.

Standing there for the national anthem in my first game at age nineteen, it was pretty clear to me that I wasn't in Alberta anymore.

Ready or not, I made my NHL debut November 20, 1946, against the Detroit Red Wings in Chicago Stadium. We lost 8-6, and I posted one assist on Pete Horecks goal. Other than that I can't tell you much about the game. Probably I had too many butterflies to record much into my memories.

During my rookie season I was the NHL's youngest defenseman, and three years later I was still the NHL's youngest defenseman.

Can't say that I felt much pressure, but I certainly understood that there were high expectations for me. Based on what they had witnessed during my junior days, the Blackhawks viewed me as a defenseman who could contribute to the offensive rush. I helped fuel higher expectations by netting eight goals in my first forty-eight NHL games.

It didn't take long before the local scribes began to pen that I had a chance to break Flash Hollett's record of twenty goals in a season by a defenseman. He had established that mark in 1944-45.

This isn't to suggest that I would spend most of my time near the opponent's net. Most of my goals came from thirty to thirty-five feet, but in that era defensemen seemed like they were tethered to their blue line. It was rare for defenseman to venture up as far as I did. When I entered the NHL, the league single-season scoring mark for a defenseman was forty points, set by Toronto's Babe Pratt in 1943-44.

Scouts viewed me as an offensive defenseman because I understood how to work with my forwards and get myself in position to score. But I always believed my first duty was to my end of the ice. Never was I a gambler on the ice. My thinking was this; I would never pinch into the offensive zone unless it was 60/40 in my favor to gain control of the puck. I always had a lot of confidence in my ability to get back and clean up my end of the ice.

When I arrived in the NHL I was probably considered an above-average skater. What's funny about that is that after I had been in the NHL for ten or fifteen seasons my first Edmonton Canadians coach, Clarence Moher, admitted to me that he almost cut me at my first junior tryout because he didn't think I could skate well enough. The fact is I had really worked at lengthening my stride in junior hockey, and by the time I got to the NHL I could move pretty well. Immediately after I was promoted to the Blackhawks there was some talk about moving me permanently to forward. At Kansas City, they had used me there and when I was called up, the man sent down was forward George Wingy Johnson. Gottselig was looking for some pop on the wing, and when I first came up he played me on line with Hank Blade and Pete Horeck. Even though I preferred defense, I kept my mouth shut because I just wanted to play in the NHL. With Hamiltons knee getting worse, it didn't take long for Gottselig to decide that I belonged on the blue line.

Having the Bentleys in Chicago helped my adjustment to the NHL tremendously. They took care of me right from the beginning. Obviously they realized my potential, but that's not why they looked after me. They looked after me because my roots were in Western Canada just like theirs were. They had come from the farming area of Delisle, Saskatchewan, and played senior hockey for the Drumheller (Alberta) Miners. That's a mining town located about sixty miles from Calgary.

When I was ten my father had taken me to a game between Drumheller and the Calgary Stampeders. Six Bentleys had played in that game, including Doug, Max and Reg who all ended up playing for the Chicago Blackhawks. (Reg ended up only playing eleven games for the Blackhawks in 1942-43 before returning to senior hockey.)

On every NHL team there was a friendly rivalry between the Western Canadian boys and the boys from back East. On the Blackhawks, we even had an East vs. West intra-squad game every year. The winning team earned the honor of scratching their names on an old piss pot. Given the intensity of those games, you would have thought we were playing for the Stanley Cup.

A few games into my career when the Bentleys invited me up to their room for a post-game beer and a sandwich at the old Manger Hotel in Boston, it was like being told you were officially part of the team. Nobody said that, but nobody had to. If the Bentleys were in your corner, you were in. Neither Bentley was taller than 5-9 and weighed more than 155 pounds soaking wet, but they were both considered among the top ten players in the league in that era. Max had been the NHL scoring leader in 1945-46, and would also win the points crown in my rookie season of 1946-47 with seventy-two points in sixty games.

Doug had won the scoring championship in 1942-43. Max was nicknamed "The Dipsy Doodle Dandy" by the press, and he was the fancier player of the two. He was a dandy passer, with slick moves and he could shoot the puck. Doug was more of a worker, moving along the boards, knocking away the puck and feeding it to his brother. They played alongside Bill Mosienko to form what was called "The Pony Line."

Mosie, as we called him, was as small as the Bentleys and he could fly down the ice. In fact, he was probably the best skater in the NHL at that time. He would whistle for the puck and Max would put the puck right on the tape of the stick. Even though the Bentleys were small, they got room to play out there because everyone in the NHL understood that if you touched the Bentleys you would have to answer to Mariucci. If there was ever a tougher player than Mariucci, I never met him. Some nights he could barely walk into the dressing room, but he would slather liniment oil on himself, pull on the sweater and would be out protecting the Bentleys. Born in Eveleth, Minnesota, Mariucci was one of the few Americans in the game during that era. He was tight with the Bentleys, on and off the ice.

Mariucci had played football and hockey at the University of Minnesota, and he was such a force as a defensive end, the NFL's Chicago Cardinals offered him a contract. But he picked hockey because it paid more. Essentially, he played hockey the same way he played football. Nobody in the league hit harder than John. In 1946-47, he broke the cheekbone of Montreal Canadiens star, Elmer Lach, with a vicious check.

One night when we were playing Detroit, the Red Wings tough guy, Doug McCaig, was pounding away on Doug Bentley as they were wrestling on the ice. Everyone in the arena could see Mariucci skating the whole length of the ice, and in the last twenty feet he doubled his fist and brought it down near the ice to prepare it for launch. When he got to McCaig he cold-cocked him with a blow to the chin that had so much power behind it that McCaig was lifted off the ice and sent flying about eight feet. In later years, former Red Wings trainer Lefty Wilson told me that when McCaigs senses started to return to him on the train-ride back to Detroit he didn't know he had been in a game.

In the NHL, with its long season, being a member of a team was like being a member of a family. You spent plenty of time with each other, on and off the ice. Humor is a staple in every dressing room. We knew each other well enough that we could rib one another constantly.

My defensive partner, in my first season, was another rookie named Ralph Nattrass. He was a steady stay-at-home kind of defenseman. Probably Gottselig figured we would compliment each other because I liked to go up and help the offense, and Ralph didn't venture too far away from his own zone. He was a couple of years older than me, but he was as green as I was in coping with the skill of NHL forwards. Whenever the coach would be hollering at us about breakdowns in the defensive coverage, Ralph would always pipe up and say, "I had my man covered." Ralph's memory of what had happened didn't always jive with my recollections of how events had transpired. It's a team game, and my philosophy was, you didn't blame anyone, you just viewed everything as a team failure. But a couple of the guys would come up to me after our team meetings, and say, "Gads, you can't let him pass all the blame to you. You have to say something." But of course I didn't.

One day at practice when we were discussing a defensive breakdown against Toronto, Nattress immediately said he had Syl Apps covered. Left wing Red Hamil , a twenty goal scorer that season, immediately chimed up, "Ralph," he said. "We are going to start calling you Mountie, because you always get your man." Everyone, including Nattress, enjoyed the laugh. That kind of give-and-take is just part of being a team member. When you are on a team, you know which buttons to push on every guy.

All of the Blackhawks bachelors lived in the Midwest Athletic Club. It was essentially a hotel on the corner of Hamlin and Madison. It had some notoriety at the time, because athletes would live there, particularly boxers, jockeys from Aqueduct raceway, and hockey players. Some of the name boxers included Rocky Marciano, Kid Gavilan and Jake LaMotta. There must have been six or seven Blackhawks players living there when I was staying there, and we really got to know LaMotta. There was always gossip about how several gangsters, or former gangsters, were also living there as well. One fellow, I do remember, was called Suitcase Sam and he was said to be the former bodyguard for Al Capone, and then for his brother Matty Capone. Suitcase Sam used to carry a machine gun in his golf bag when he golfed with Capones; at least that's how the story went.

Living there for an extended period, I got to know many of the regulars who lived there, and some of them were hoods. The whole second floor was set-up for illegal gambling. The funny thing was that several members of the Chicago police force, including officers, also lived at that hotel as well. Even though there was gambling going on there at all hours of the night, no one ever bothered the athletes. There seemed to be a code that everyone who lived there respected the others who lived there.

Moving to Chicago was like moving to another world for me. Calgary really was a small town by comparison. Everyday I would look at the skyline and shake my head. The Chicago Board of Trade building, built in 1930, was forty-five stories. Chicago had many buildings taller than any I had known in my hometown. I was awe-struck by this thriving, colorful city with vibrant people and characters.

One of the most colorful Chicago characters was William Sianis, a Greek immigrant who owned the famous Billy Goat Tavern. Many knew the tavern because it is believed the place was the model for the famous Saturday Night Live skit featuring John Belushi yelling, "Cheeseburger, Cheeseburger, Cheeseburger." The late Chicago columnist, Mike Royko, also wrote frequently about the establishment, now located on Michigan Avenue and owned by Sianis nephew.

When I arrived in Chicago in 1946, the Billy Goat Tavern was on Madison Avenue, across from Chicago Stadium. William Sianis was the sole owner, and he was the slickest promoter this side of P.T. Barnum.

According to the story that Sianis passed along to his heirs, he bought a bar named the Lincoln Tavern with a bad check for just over $200. He made enough money the first weekend to go to the bank and take care of his bad check. He kept the original name until an accident in front of his establishment emancipated a goat, which Sianis quickly adopted and named Murphy. The goat quickly became the bars signature and Sianis quickly re-named his bar The Billy Goat Tavern.

When you went in there, he had a sawdust floor and two or three goats would be walking among the customers.

All the Blackhawks knew Sianis because he used to buy tickets to games, and bring the goat into the game. Sooner or later, they would kick the goat out and Sianis would come back by himself. He loved all the attention, and the Blackhawks had reason to tolerate his nightly ritual of bringing the goat. He had taken his goat to Wrigley Field to see the 1945 World Series, and the ushers had thrown out Murphy because they said he had a pungent odor. As they were leaving, or so the story goes, Sianis placed a hex on the Cubs. The Cubs lost that series, and still to this day haven't won a World Series. After the series, Sianis had written a note to Cubs owner P.K. Wrigley saying simply, "Who stinks now?"

Sianis never missed an opportunity for promoting his tavern. In 1944, when the Republican convention was at the stadium, he put a sign on his bar that read No Republicans allowed.

When the Blackhawks would go in there, Sianis was always trying to work some practical joke. He always had a package sitting on the bar, and when a new patron would walk in Sianis would ask him to pick it up and guess what it weighed. He made up some story about how he needed to know how much postage money he needed to give to the employee who was taking it the post office. When the patron picked up the box, he would be given a mild electrical shock and everyone in the bar would howl.

On the night I took my parents into the tavern for the first time, Sianis brought over an old flute and asked my mother to try and squeeze a couple of notes out of it. When she blew on it, some black soot would come out and cover her face. It wasn't enough for her to notice, but more than enough to get a few laughs from the other patrons. "Why is everyone laughing?" she said to me. "I told you I couldn't play this thing."

Chicago was always fun, even on nights there were no games. When we weren't playing hockey, many of us would be at Chicago Stadium watching shows or boxing. Chicago Stadium always got big names and big events. In my first few years in the NHL, I saw plenty of stars. I remember skater Sonja Henie was a regular there, and I saw her quite a bit. I remember a young Sammy Davis Jr. and a young Lena

Horne appearing at Chicago Stadium before they became national stars. I met actor Dennis Morgan and even had my picture taken with him.

Maybe the most memorable event from that era was seeing Jake Raging Bull LaMotta fight Sugar Ray Robinson in February, 1951. We lived in the same building as LaMotta and we knew him pretty well. He had beat Robinson (in 1943) the first time and there was plenty of hope in Chicago that LaMotta could take him again. LaMotta had won the title in 1949 over Marcel Cerdan, and had rallied from behind to defeat Laurent Dauthuille to hold the championship in 1950. Everyone was waiting for the fight with Robinson. He was thirty when he fought Robinson that night in Chicago, and he seemed much older when it was over. The fight was called in the 13th round with LaMotta still on his feet, but looking as bad as a man could look while still breathing and standing. It was a great fight, certainly the best pro bout I've ever seen, but the end result was LaMotta lost his championship.

As friends of LaMotta, several Blackhawks were ushered into LaMotta's dressing room. But as soon as I entered the room, I wanted out of there. I will never forget the image of seeing LaMotta's wife cradling his head in her arms. She was wearing a white dress and it was soaked in blood. His face looked like ground up hamburger. He boxed three more years after that, but never had much success.

Perhaps I learned as much about life as I learned about hockey in my first few seasons in the NIIL.

Maybe what I learned from Mariucci, the Bentleys, and maybe even LaMotta, is how tough you have to be to survive in professional sports, and maybe how fleeting success can be.

In my first season in 1946-47, I led all NHL defenseman in goals with eight. That was two more goals than Gordie Howe scored that season; a fact that I have never let him forget, even to this day.

After staying in contention for the playoffs for a while, we ended up falling to the basement that season. If we had just won more often, my rookie season couldn't have been much better. Whether it was true or not I can't say, but Gottselig told reporters in several cities that I had joined Charley Conacher, Busher Jackson and former Chicago player Mush Marsh as the only junior-age players who had jumped from the amateur ranks to the NHL in one season.

Later that season, Gottselig was quoted in the newspaper as saying I was ahead of where former Chicago standout Earl Seibert was at when he first broke into the NHL.

That 1946-47 season was known as the year of the rookies because Chicago had me, and Toronto boasted Howie Meeker, and Boston had Mark Marquess, and Montreal had Blonde Leo Gravelle. Scoring twenty-seven goals to put himself among the league leaders, Meeker was named NHL Rookie of the Year. That certainly didn't bother me because I thought I was on a pretty good hockey club that was going to improve. As it turned out, I was wrong about that. But in hindsight I wouldn't have traded my early years in Chicago to have played for any other team.

Many folks remember that the Blackhawks didn't draw particularly well in the 1950s, but when I got there the building was always hopping. A then record crowd of 20,004 fans showed up to witness Emile Francis make his NHL debut on February 23, 1947.

Coincidentally, my first season in the NHL turned out to be the last for Boston Bruins standout, Dit Clapper. As the season was winding down, each NHL team paid homage to Clapper's career with a short pre-game ceremony. Clapper was an avid hunter and the Blackhawks decided to give him a new shotgun as a going-away gift. They choose me to make the presentation because I was only a couple of months old when Clapper launched his Hall of Fame career with the Bruins. When we met at center ice I just said, "Congratulations, Mr. Clapper, on your long career." Maybe when Clapper stared at the nineteen year-old in front of him he was reminded what he was like at my age. He smiled, and said, " Son, I just hope you can play twenty seasons like I did." At the time neither one of us probably believed that was possible. But we were wrong.

Chapter 4

Maybe what was implied was more important than what was actually written in the first letter I penned to Edna after being called up by the Blackhawks.

In a letter dated December 6, 1946, seventeen days after I was called, up I told Edna how surprised I was that so many girls were excited about meeting a member of the Blackhawks. And they don't even care what you look like, so I'm right in there, I wrote.

Even though officially we weren't viewing ourselves as a couple, I wrote honey in the letter and then crossed it out with a note that I had slipped. Near the end of the letter, I also mentioned the radio was playing, "There I've Said It Again," by Vaughn Monroe. "Remember when that song was playing when we came back from at date on the bus?" I wrote. Does this sound like someone who doesn't think this relationship was going to work?

Before I left for my first National Hockey League training camp in Regina in 1946, Edna and I both decided that we should be free to see other people. In hindsight, Edna believes we showed a maturity beyond our years because we both realized that we were too young to make a commitment, particularly with me heading off to pursue a career that would take me away from home for six or seven months every year.

Even though I wrote her regularly from training camp and Kansas City, Edna says she figured we didn't have much long-term potential because I was heading off to Chicago where their would probably be more girls than I could shake my hockey stick at.

But truthfully I believed we had a future. I had this sweet memory about a warm summer's evening in Edmonton in 1948. I remember kissing Edna goodnight and climbing aboard the last streetcar just before midnight to get back across town. She was a good-looking young gal, and she was smart as could be. She was working for Canada Income Tax. I remember thinking she's the one for me. I knew it right then. It was a wonderful feeling. I can still remember my contentment, even though it was more than a half century ago.

This was the girl I had taken home to meet my parents in Calgary. This was the girl my mother had given my scrapbooks to keep up for me while I was playing in Edmonton. This was the girl I thought I was going to marry, even if she had her doubts.

That's not to say we didn't have some ups and downs in the seven years I knew her before we married. It was like a long distance romance even when I came home for the summer because I went back to Calgary to play semi-pro baseball. A lot of NHL players did that because the money was darn good. By playing in a tournament every weekend, you could earn a couple hundred dollars and more if you won. Gordie Howe used to play for the Saskatoon team.

The competition in Western Canada was good enough that most teams attracted players from Arizona and California, including some major league prospects. I played on the same team with the late Glen Gorbous, who played briefly in the major leagues with the Cincinnati Reds and the Philadelphia Phillies. Gorbous was from Drumheller, Alberta and he had an arm from the outfield that could rival any of today's guns. My position was catcher, at least it was until Blackhawk's president Bill Tobin found out about my summer hobby. He made me switch to the outfield, saying catching was too dangerous.

It is fair to suggest that I enjoyed my summers of baseball almost as much as my winters of hockey. One summer, early in my NHL career, I had too many good times and I ended up eating and drinking my way to 210 pounds; that was about twenty pounds heavier than my playing weight. When I got to training camp in North Bay, the stops and starts in the opening days of practice almost killed me. At the moment when I couldn't have felt any worse at that training camp I vowed I would never again allow myself to get out of shape, and I never did.

When I wasn't playing baseball I would drive up to see Edna in Edmonton, but honestly there wasn't as much time to see her as you would think for a guy who technically had six months off every summer. After baseball tournaments, the guys would want to go out for a beer or two. Maybe I wasn't ready to get married or maybe time just marched by too quickly, but we knew each other seven years before we got married.

Edna was right when she says there were some

times in that seven years when our future would seem doubtful to anyone from the outside looking in.

Once, one of my buddies talked me into taking one his friends to a Louis Armstrong concert at the Edmonton Coliseum. What I didn't know was that one of Edna's friends had talked her into going, and she had spotted me there with another woman.

When I went to see her the next day she had all of my scrapbooks together to give to me, and she gave me one of those looks that suggested she never wanted to see me again. "You were at the Louis Armstrong concert last night with someone," she said, not revealing the source of her information.

"Who said they saw me there?" I said, probably thinking I was going to plead mistaken identity. I just kept digging myself deeper into a hole, and by the end of the conversation I was buried with all of my scrapbooks. That took me a few days, maybe even a week, to win back Edna with some heart-felt apologies.

I can't say why I knew that Edna was the one for me, nor can I tell you why I waited so long. Edna has letters, written in the 1951-52 season, in which I lament that we hadn't gotten married the summer before.

In that season, however, I told Edna that I had purchased her an engagement ring, but insisted she had to come to Chicago to get it. I arranged for her to take a train from Edmonton, through Saskatoon where she would meet up with Doug Bentley's wife in Regina. They would arrive together.

Once she got to Chicago, Edna wondered what I was up to because there was no mention of the ring. One evening during her stay we went to a team party, and all the guys were there. The Bentleys, Gus Bodnar and his wife were there, so was Black Jack Stewart, who had been traded to Chicago in 1950, a couple of years after his famous fight with John Mariucci. Harry Lumley, the goalie I had beaten for my favorite goal with two seconds left in regular as a rookie, was also there. He had come over from Detroit in the same trade.

When we showed up, Edna thought it was kind of peculiar that there was champagne and roses at a team gathering.

The guys slipped out of the room and I slipped the ring on Edna's finger, and that night we officially began an adventure that has lasted more than a half century.

One other event happened on that trip that Edna and I still laugh about to this day. I had a friend in Chicago, actually he was a fan, and often I would mention in my letters that he would bring his daughters along on our outings. Edna just assumed that his daughters were youngsters, and she was rather surprised, to say the least, when she met them and realized that the oldest was essentially my age and it was pretty clear that she had some interest in me.

Actually, my old friend, had told me that his daughter was interested, and I had told him that I liked being around her as a friend but I had a girl back home.

Edna accepted that story, but when we were out at a tavern in Berwynn, Illinois with some teammates and friends, the girl in question happened to be there. And as fate would have it, Edna ended up in the washroom at the same time with the girl and a friend. They didn't know Edna was in the stall when they started talking.

"What do you think of Bill Gadsby's girlfriend?" one of them asked my friend's daughter.

"Strictly from Hicksville," she said.

At the time, Edna was quite upset. But Gus Bodnar's wife saw something was wrong, and when Edna explained what had happened, she told her not to worry that the daughter was spoiled and simply jealous.

Now, "Strictly from Hicksville" has simply become a joke between us, and our friends. Gordie and Colleen Howe have heard the story enough that a couple of times Colleen has sent letters to Edna and addressed them on the front, "Strictly from Hicksville."

Edna and I became friends with Gordie and Colleen before we actually played together for the Red Wings. We used to play semi-pro baseball against each other. Gordie and Colleen became friends with Edna and I in 1954, at Lake Waskesiu in Northern Saskatchewan. Gordie had mentioned that he went up there in the summer, and I told him maybe we would see him up there. Edna had vacationed there as a youngster, and she wanted to go back.

Coincidentally, Johnny Bower, who would later become a Hall of Fame goaltender, owned a concession stand there. The interesting aspect of lakes in northern Saskatchewan is that no matter how warm it is outside the lake is still freezing. It could be 80 degrees outside, but that water would send you into shock.

I can't say I truly understood how frigid that water was until Gordie suggested that we take a swim up there. He took a running dive right into the lake. My thinking was that if Gordie Howe could do that, I could do it as well. I dove right in and the water was so cold that my heart almost stopped. After twenty seconds, I came running out of that water to find Gordie laughing uncontrollably. We've been close friends ever since.

Edna likes to point out that when she met Colleen for the first time the circumstances pointed out the difference in their personalities. At the time Colleen was golfing and Edna was picking strawberries

However as different as their personalities may have been, Colleen and Edna, and Gordie and I have been friends for about five decades. When I was playing in Detroit and we would have games on Christmas Day, we always got our two families together to spend the holidays together. The Howes introduced many of our long-time friends to us. You couldn't find two better friends than the Howes.

Colleen's willingness to play tough in the business world has earned her some criticism, but the Colleen Howe we know is simply a generous, kind-hearted person. Most of the stories of her generosity never became public, but I can tell you that she was a woman who always made sure that the Red Wings wives were taken care of.

Edna and I remember well when one of my former teammates didn't bring his paycheck home to his family. It was Colleen who showed up on the doorstep with groceries and money to pay the bills. Nobody knew that except that player's wife and us. Colleen never wanted anyone to know.

Before Edna and I were married, we met for pre-marriage counseling with a minister and even though we had known each other for seven years he asked us many questions that made us think about how our marriage was going to work. How many children did we want? Where did we want to live? Who was going to handle the money?

On that last question, I piped up and said, "I will

let her take care of the money for one year, and if she does a good job then she can always be in charge of that."

In that season with the Blackhawks, I made $11,000 and Edna managed to save $7,000. She has been overseeing our finances ever since.

In all marriages, the first few years can seem like a carnival ride full of twists and turns that keep you both excited and nervous about what will happened next. But when you are also dealing with the uncertainty of being a professional athlete, it makes the roller coaster effect even more pronounced.

When we look back at the first couple of years of marriage in Chicago, we mostly laugh at the good times, like the night the crazy fans of Chicago attempted to hurl a fish onto the ice and it landed in Edna's lap.

We also laugh about the night that Vic Lynn volunteered to watch Brenda so Edna and I could go out for supper on the town. At the start of the 1953-54 season, Edna and I moved into the Athletic Club for a week until our house was ready. I wanted to take Edna out for a supper on the town, but she was nervous about leaving our four-month old with a babysitter. "Don't worry," I said. "I got Vic Lynn to take care of Brenda." Vic had three children of his own, and he knew a little about taking care of a baby. He said he would be glad to do it.

At the time Edna and I had an English baby carriage, a very distinctive model, and one you weren't going to see in downtown Chicago. That's only important because when Edna and I came home, that carriage was parked outside the door of the Athletic Club's bar. "He didn't take Brenda into the bar, did he?" Edna said. "Well I hope so because she's not in the baby carriage," I said. When we entered the bar, we found Vic in a booth, next to a man who was bouncing Brenda on his knee. Vic started to apologize, saying he hoped that we didn't mind if he brought Brenda down here. No problem, I said, amused by the sight of my daughter being played with by Matty Capone, brother of the infamous Chicago mobster, Al Capone. Edna had no idea who he was, and when I told her who Matty Capone was her knees just buckled.

Matty was really just a small-time hoodlum, compared to his brother, and he had a habit I won't forget. He always sat with his hand over his drink because he feared that someone might try to slip something in it.

Even though I spent nine seasons in Chicago and it seemed like a second home to me, Edna will tell you that she had her best time in New York after we traded. We were the youngest couple on the Chicago team, and after the trade to Rangers we were the oldest couple on the team. New York was better for Edna because in Chicago we lived out by ourselves and she would have to come into the games early with me. In New York we all lived in Glen Oaks Village and the guys would come to the game together. The wives would come a couple hours later, and we would all go home together. Gump and Doreen Worsley, Andy and Merle Bathgate, Harry and Marilyn Howell, and Edna and I were all great friends, and still are to this day. In New York we took in Broadway plays, and I got to take the two oldest girls down to skate at Rockefeller Center.

You were definitely somebody when you played in New York. Ed Sullivan even mentioned in his column once that the Rangers Gadsbys' were expecting the stork. Actress Kim Novak watched a Rangers game, and was quoted in the newspaper as saying she liked to watch that fellow Gadsby playing hockey. New York was important to us because that's where we were playing when three of our four children were born. We call our New York years our productive years because we had a child every two years. The funny thing is that all of our kids were born in Edmonton in the off-season. Talk about good timing. We were very happy in New York.

At the time the trade occurred, I wasn't thrilled with the idea of going to Manhattan. Five minutes before the train was supposed to pull out of Illinois Central station, Frank Eddols came up to me and said that I'd been traded to the New York Rangers. "You have to go this afternoon," Eddols said. Considering how ticked off I was, it was probably fortunate for both Eddols and I that all I said was, "I'm not going to go anywhere this afternoon."

By the time I got home to tell Edna, I had already formulated a theory about why I had been dealt to the New York Rangers. The season before, Ivan was coaching the strong Detroit Red Wings team which was overflowing with talent, and in one heated game, I had nailed some Detroit player with a rough check.

As I skated by the bench, Ivan was giving me the business. "You have a bad hockey club," he screamed. "And all you can do is try to hurt my players."

Probably I should have just told him to shut up. But instead, I stopped, turned around, and yelled, "You don't even coach this team. You are just a gate opener."

When he became general manager of the Blackhawks a year later, I wondered whether he

remembered that episode. I never knew for sure
whether my insult had entered into his thinking, but the
Blackhawks didn't have much reason to trade me,
considering I was their captain.

Once anger subsided, my goal became to squeeze
more money out of the Rangers. When I told Rangers
GM Frank Boucher, I was thinking about quitting
unless he gave me a raise, he told me I would have to
live with the contract I had in Chicago.

In the end, he did give me some extra money.
But I was going to go no matter how much he gave me.
Life had taught me that you had to deal with many
obstacles along the way, and being traded to another
hockey team wasn't the worst thing that had ever
happened in my life. Not even close.

Chapter 5

One crisp morning in September 1952, I woke up in Edmonton thinking I was suffering from the worst hangover I had ever had. Two days later, I woke up in an Ottawa Hospital with a doctor telling me I had contracted polio. The diagnosis was almost more unbelievable than it was scary.

Here I was feeling like I was on top of the world, having just spent four glorious months with my new bride. We were married June 16, 1952, and planned a two-week honeymoon, intending to drive all the way to Las Vegas. We stopped in beautiful, Coeur D Alene, Idaho and never made it to Vegas.

My golf driving range in Edmonton was doing a healthy business. And I was about to start my seventh NHL season. Life couldn't have been better, or so I thought. In October, I got ready to head to training camp in North Bay, Ontario. The plan was that I would go to training camp and Edna would meet me in Chicago.

The night before I let my friends take me out for a going away gathering. I was still drinking back then, so when I woke up the next morning feeling awful, I thought the drink was paying me back. Even Edna presumed I had a hangover.

In those days, you didn't dare miss even a day of training camp. Regardless of how poorly I was feeling, I knew I had to board that plane for Toronto. You were always worried about someone stealing your job. Even though I had been in the league for seven seasons, I never took my place for granted. None of us did.

On the flight to Toronto, it was clear this was no hangover. Two or three times I vomited on the plane, and my shoulders and muscles ached as if an unknown assailant had been beating me with a two-by-four. My neck ached. Chills ran through me.

Blackhawks president, Bill Tobin, met me at the airport and as soon as he saw me he said, " You look terrible. We have to get you to a doctor."

We took a limousine to North Bay, and we had to stop a couple of times so I could throw up. The doctor who examined me in North Bay looked alarmed.

"You have the symptoms of polio," he said.

That just scared me to death. They crammed me into an ambulance to transport me to a hospital in Ottawa where more elaborate testing could be done. A doctor came in and confirmed that I had polio. As I recall, he explained to me that I had forty-nine polio cells in my spinal fluid and that people with fifty-one polio-infected cells end up paralyzed. Needless to say, I was right on the borderline.

Telling Edna I had polio was probably more difficult than hearing the news myself. I knew she would be scared to death, particularly being two time zones away from me. What neither of us knew at the time was that Edna was expecting our first child,

Brenda. It's probably better we didn't know because it probably would have compounded our fear. This was at a time when polio was at an epidemic stage in Western Canada. The mystery of the disease made it seem more ominous than it already was. The medical community knew this was a communicable disease, yet no one seemed to know how it was spread and why some of the stricken recovered fully, while others became paralyzed. or died.

Edna and I still shake our heads about how my medical condition was dealt with by the team in those days. If a NHL athlete is injured or becomes ill today, the team immediately flies in his family members to be with him.

Back then Tobin simply called Edna and said there was no need to worry because I was receiving good care and the prognosis was good. He said I was in isolation, and I really didn't need visitors. I just needed rest. That was just the way life was handled back then, when you were a pro athlete.

As the days wore on, my health and strength started to return. The doctor said I was lucky because he believed I was going to make a full recovery. My hospital stay was probably ten days to two weeks. I probably lost fifteen pounds over that period. When Edna came to Chicago, she was stunned by how thin I was.

We weren't complaining. We were thankful for my health. Two teenagers who were working for me at my driving range in Edmonton in 1952, came down with polio at the same time I had it and they have paralysis to this day.

Edna says my guardian angel was looking after me during that period, and that wasn't the first or last time that I felt as if I had been blessed when I stood at the doorstep of tragedy.

Many young Canadian boys with dreams of a National Hockey League career have had their plans sunk by a major injury or a flaw in their game. My hunch is that I'm one of the few whose career was almost sunk before it began by a torpedo from a German U-boat.

War was in the air in the summer of 1939, when my mother and I steamed across the Atlantic to visit her relatives in Southport Lancashire, England about twenty miles from Liverpool. Around the globe there was fear about Nazi aggression, but if my mother was worried, she didn't show it. And a holiday across the ocean was a grand adventure to an eleven year-old boy from Calgary. The thought that we could find ourselves in harm's way never entered our mind.

We stayed in England for three months, and my mother had booked our passage on the Montreal-bound 13,581-ton passenger liner, S.S. Athenia, well in advance of our September 1st departure from Glasgow, Scotland. She could not have anticipated that Germany would have invaded Poland, and World War II would be launched two days into our journey.

Officially, World War II was about ten hours old on the night of September 3rd, but presumably most of the passengers on the Athenia probably didn't know. It was a beautiful evening, with calm seas, and crisp early fall air. By eight o'clock, the 1,103 passengers and 303 crewmembers were all settled into their routines. Many of the passengers were still preparing for supper, but my mother was already insisting that it was time for me to go to the bed. By about 8:45 p.m. she had me settled into my bunk. Fifteen minutes later a blast launched me right out of my berth. What followed was the most chaotic scene I've ever witnessed. Our sleeping compartment was well below deck, and as mother pulled me into the hallway, we found ourselves in the midst of people scrambling in every direction to get reunited with their families. We were all bumping into each other in our efforts to reach the top deck of the ship. Panic was sketched into the faces. You don't ever forget seeing that level of fright on a human face.

No one seemed to know what had happened. The assumption was that there had been an explosion in the engine room. A boiler, maybe. Knowing the cause of the blast didn't carry the same urgency as climbing to the deck of the ship. As I grew older, I realized how terrified my mother must have been in those harrowing moments. But at the time, she showed only calmness to her youngest son. To be honest, I don't remember being afraid. Less than a month before, I had reached my 12th birthday. I was still too young to appreciate the danger of the moment. At that age, you look to your parent to determine what emotion you should have, and my mother gave me no reason to worry.

Once we reached the top deck, the situation wasn't like a scene from the movie Titanic. There seemed to be enough lifeboats, and the crew was packing passengers into the crafts in an orderly fashion and launching them into the Atlantic as rapidly as humanly possible. However, we were jammed into the boats; there must have been fifty in our dingy.

I don't remember much about being in the boat. It was pitch black by then and the night air had turned rather damp and cold. People weren't talking much. I remember there wasn't anything to eat, but some people had tea. Funny what you remember. And funny how English folks would end up with tea on a lifeboat.

I can't recall how long we were bobbing up and down in seas that seemed to be becoming rougher as the time ticked away. Maybe we were out there only a couple of hours, but it seemed longer. Those of us in the lifeboats certainly didn't know that the captain had radioed a SOS call and the Norwegian ship, Knut Nelson, had been in that area and responded almost immediately. Through official reports later on, we found out that six ships actually aided in the rescue, including two other merchant ships, City of Flint and Southern Cross. The other three responding vessels were the British destroyers, Electra, Escort and Fame. I couldn't tell you what ship we ended up on.

It wasn't until we were back on English soil that we discovered that 118 passengers died in the sinking of Athenia. It wasn't until we were back on English soil that we understood that we had been torpedoed by a German submarine.

The complete story wouldn't come out until after the war, when German officials gave their accounts at the Nuremberg trials about what happened that night, and about how the Reich military establishment had attempted to cover up the incident.

According to official military documents, the U-boat that sunk the Athenia was the U-30 commanded by 28-year-old Oberleutnant Fritz-Julius Lemp.

After the state of war had been officially declared, the German naval command had issued orders to all submarines that gave them permission to attack all enemy shipping without provocation. However, the command apparently was given that the German captains were instructed to follow the Prize Rules of Sea Engagement. The important tenets of those rules, as they pertained to the sinking of the Athenia, included Lemp's failure to warn the merchant ship of his intention to sink it and his decision not to.

Testimony, after the war, suggested that Lemp had spotted the Athenia at about 8:40 p.m. and had made no effort to warn of his pending attack. Instead of firing a shot across the bow as was required by Prize Rules, he put a torpedo squarely into the ship's port side where it was able to penetrate the engine room. According to a report, that is now listed on U-Boat.com, Lemp actually fired three torpedoes at the Athenia.

He fired two shots back-to-back, but one of those misfired and the U-30 had to submerge out of fear that the misfired torpedo would circle back, and hone in on the U-boat. When he returned to periscope depth, he saw that the Athenia was surprisingly still afloat, although listing badly. He fired another torpedo that missed the stricken ship. Some military historians theorize the missed shot is why some survivors believed that the Germans had fired on the lifeboats.

Lemp's violation of the rules of sea warfare was made more grievous by his decision not to surface and check on the condition of the survivors.

According to German military records, he didn't even report the incident until September 27th when he returned to port. He had not reported the sinking when he had radioed in on September 14th to report damage from an encounter with two military vessels and to ask permission to leave a wounded man in Iceland.

This was the first ship sunk during the war, and it was major news all over the world. The Germans knew that the Lemp's U-30 was the only U-boat operating Northeast of Ireland, where the sinking had occurred. Knowing how the sinking of the Luisitania had brought the allies together in World War I, the Germans schemed immediately to place blame for the sinking elsewhere.

Lemp told his German superiors that the Athenia was zigzagging in a defensive posture without any running lights, and he thought he spotted guns on the side. Lemp said he presumed the vessel to be an armed merchant ship. The fallacy of his statement was evident because it was a clear night on the seas and there were certainly no guns on this ship. The Athenia had more than 1,000 passengers, and it would have risked the safety of all of them to be steaming across the ocean without lights. Of course we had lights.

Whether they believed him or not wasn't as important to the German brass as the plan for denying blame in the court of world opinion. During World War II, the Germans always had the propaganda machine churning at all times. About a month after Lemp had told the Germans the truth, a German newspaper came out with a story that stated the British had sunk their own ship with the hope of bringing the Americans into the war.

U-30 logbooks were re-written to exclude reference to the Athenia, and even the personal diary accounts of Admiral Karl Doenitz listed all of U-30 action, except it's attack on the Athenia.

Lemp wasn't court-martialed for his action, and he eventually ended up in command of the U-110. That boat was crippled in a depth charge attack, and forced to surface. Realizing the British were going to ram the submarine, Lemp ordered his crewmembers to abandon ship. When Lemp and the Germans were away from the submarine, Lemp realized that the sub wasn't going to sink and the British were going to capture the sub.

He attempted to swim back to his submarine. It's unknown whether he drowned or was killed by British gunfire, but he was never seen again. (The U-30 had several different commanders during the war, and the Athenia turned out to be just one of seventeen ships sunk by the submarine. The submarine was scuttled at the conclusion of the war.)

The Germans, not wanting others to enter the war, made it a point after the sinking of the Athenia, not to disregard the rules of sea warfare. Just four days after the Athenia was sent to the Ocean floor, the U-33 German submarine encountered a merchant ship, Olivegrove, steaming toward Britain. With Captain James Barnetson in charge, the Olivegrove was coming from Cuba where it picked up a cargo of sugar. Spotting the German U-boat, Barnetson tried vainly to lose the sub by throwing up a smoke screen. However, U-33 just kept moving closer. Rather than sink the Olivegrove immediately, U-33 commander Hans-Wilhelm von Dresky fired a torpedo across the bow. Immediately the British captain turned off his engines, leaving his boat helpless in the water.

Von Dresky waited for all the lifeboats to have rowed clear of the ship before he sunk it with one torpedo into the engine room.

The U-33 then surfaced, and Von Dresky invited Barnetson aboard. After the two had shook hands, the German captain apologized for the sinking, saying he was simply doing his duty at a time of war. He told the British captain that he had radioed plainly to allied ships to report that survivors from a British supply ship were in lifeboats. He provided the precise coordinates of their location.

The British captain thanked Dresky and then

headed back to his lifeboats. According to the British captain's report, the U-33 boat stayed in the vicinity for nine hours to make sure that help was really on the way. Von Dresky's humane treatment of the Olivegrove's did not spare him from a tragic fate. He was killed in combat when the U-33 was sunk by depth charges five months later in the Firth of Clyde.

That civil level of wartime conduct wasn't seen the night the sinking of the Athenia occurred.

The reason so much is known about what happened to the Athenia that night is that one important German survivor came forward after the war.

In all the German efforts to cover up the event, they couldn't do anything about German sailor Adolf Schmidt, who was the wounded U-30 crewman who had been put ashore in Iceland. He had been captured by the Brits when they occupied the island in 1940, but Lemp told the German brass not to worry about Schmidt because he had sworn an oath of secrecy before leaving U-30. He honored that oath throughout his capture, interrogation and imprisonment as a POW. When the war was over, Schmidt decided the oath was no longer valid. At the Nuremberg trials, he provided the truth of what really happened the night of September 3, 1939.

Of course none of these stories were known to me, or to my mother, on the night of the sinking or years after, for that matter. Only later in life did I discover the truth of what had occurred that night.

Our concern, once we landed, was getting word to my father, who we knew would simply be frantic when hearing about the sinking. With the threat of war imminent, we couldn't tell my father what ship we would be on, but he knew approximately when we would set sail. It was days before anyone knew who had survived and who had died. With four daughters of my own, I can just imagine how it must have been for my father, not to know for days what had happened to his wife and child.

Needless to say we didn't get on another ship as soon as we returned to England. We stayed there another two months before we got back on another passenger ship.

Our stay there during the war just seemed like part of the adventure. We were given gas masks, and I remember helping fill sand bags to be used as part of the coastal defense. We heard the German bombers going overhead, and just hoped they weren't headed to Liverpool. Their destination always turned out to be London.

A government-ordered blackout was in effect throughout England, and I can remember black paper plastered over all of the windows. Some people chose to cover their windows with a couple coats of black paint. I remember helping paint those windows black. No one cared how neat it was. You just slopped on the black paint enough not to allow even a hint of light to seep in. Nobody violated the blackout rules.

When we finally boarded another ship, I wasn't really scared. Probably I should have been, but I was so young that I didn't appreciate the danger. Again my mother was probably petrified, but she never showed it. She was as cool as she could be.

Once we returned home, it was clear that the sinking had a dramatic effect on my mother. She wouldn't talk about it, and she didn't like me to talk about it. Even when reporters would ask me about it

once I got to the NHL, I didn't say a whole lot.
Whenever I said anything about it in the newspapers, it
bothered my mother. Out of respect for her, I stopped
talking about it completely at some point in my career.

Still today, I haven't talked much about it.
Maybe I've purposely blanked that out of my memory,
preferring not to dwell on a night when others in my
circumstance lost their lives. There was no physical
injuries the night of the sinking, but it's impossible to
say that I came out of that without some scars.

Likewise, my bout with polio left no lasting
physical effects. In fact, that 1952-53 season was among
the most memorable of my career. The Blackhawks
made the playoffs for the first time in my career, and I
played in the NHL All-Star game for the first time. At
the end of the season, I was named to the NHL's
second-team All-Star team. Life is strange. In October,
I'm lying in a bed wondering whether I will live or be
crippled and six months later I'm honored as one of the
NHL's best players.

The All-Star defensemen in 1952-53
were Red Kelly and Doug Harvey on the first-team and
Tim Horton and me on the second team. That's pretty
good company.

When the stories of my battle with polio or the
Asthenia incident surfaced during my career, more than
one sportswriter suggested that my playing on the edge
was a result of my brushes with death in the Atlantic
and in the polio ward. One writer in Boston wrote that
I was a fatalist. But honestly I didn't think about all
that much when I was young.

It does seem that I have had more than my fair
share of intimate contact with tragedy. Shortly after I
retired from hockey, I buried my close friend and

business partner, Clarence Moher, who had been my first junior coach in Edmonton. He and I were partners in the driving range, and I was accustomed to hearing from him at all hours of the night. If cell phones had been invented during his life, he would have had the largest bill in phone history. He was a bachelor and he loved to gab.

That's why I wasn't alarmed when he called me late one night until I realized that he was struggling to catch his breath. It was clear something was very wrong, and by the time I called Edna to the phone I was halfway out the door.

When I arrived at Clarence's apartment, I got the superintendent to use the master key to let me in. Clarence had the chain-lock on the door, but when I peeked in I could see him lying on the floor. It took me just a second to decide to break down the door. I probably hit that door as hard as I hit Horton that night in Toronto. I hit it hard enough that I threw out my back, and ended up in the hospital in traction. That was the farthest thing from my mind as I reached Clarence and found him dead with the phone and his nitroglycerin tablets on his chest. He was just forty-eight years old.

In 1971, death visited me again when former Chicago teammate George Gee collapsed and died of a heart attack while sitting next to me on the bench during a Red Wings oldtimers' game. He was just forty-nine.

As I grew older, I started to reflect about the events of my life, and certainly it caused me to shudder a few nights before I went to sleep. It does seem as if I have had a guardian angel, particularly that night when the Nazi sub commander fired on a helpless passenger ship.

Some parents, up on the deck listening to the music, couldn't get to the children below after the explosion. The hallways started to fill with water within minutes of the explosion. Clearly, I had been lucky that my mother was there to lead me up the stairs.

Perhaps it is possible that my ability to play through so many injuries reflected my relief at having survived that ordeal. What's a few cuts and bruises picked up in a hockey game after you have survived in those circumstances?

It was just recently, while lying in bed, that I became overwhelmed by the sense of how lucky I had been during my life. Hockey players truly don't fear anything when they are playing on the ice. They don't think about the possibility of a major injury. All the time the pucks would go whizzing past my head it never occurred me to think that if one of those had struck me in the temple, I could have died.

Likewise, through all of those years, it really hadn't struck me about how close I had to come to dying on at least three separate occasions.

My bout with polio came within months of Jonas Salk proving that his polio vaccine would work, but it would be two more years before it was in widespread use. Some folks we knew died from polio. One of my former teammates was Billy McNeill, who played for the Detroit Red Wings in the 1950s and early 1960s. He was in Edmonton and we knew him well. His wife was expecting, and she went to the same doctor that Edna did. She was stricken with polio, and she died. Her baby did survive.

Certainly I came through that ordeal and the Athenia sinking with a greater appreciation of life and health.

The event that made me think about how lucky I was didn't involve the polio disease or the tragedy on the Atlantic. It involved an event that occurred when I was about fourteen years old. My father was in charge of the baggage department for the Canadian Pacific Railway, and I would get to drive the truck on some of his deliveries. On one such delivery, my father carted baggage upstairs in a downtown Calgary office building while I waited on the street. I was just standing on the walkway, watching cars driving past when this massive chunk of concrete grazed my shirt and landed inches away from feet. My estimate is that it weighed about 30 to 40 pounds. It had broken away from the building four stories up and came within a foot or less of killing me right there on the streets of Calgary.

When I think about the whap sound the block of cement made as it crashed to the earth that day, all I can think about is how lucky I've been in my life. Like Edna says, it's as if someone has long been in charge of looking after my well being.

Chapter 6

For a fleeting moment, after stunning Tim Horton with a thunderous bodycheck in 1956-57, the thought crossed my mind that I might have killed him.

He was sprawled motionless on the Maple Leaf Gardens' ice with one glove off and his stick several feet away from his body. He looked like a casualty of war, blood seeping from one ear and the corner of his mouth. It was a scariest moment of my career. I never hit anyone with greater force than I nailed Horton that night. I caught him with his head down just inside the blue line. Funny thing was, I never felt the thud. Usually when you caught someone good you experienced the pain as well. Usually, it was a head-on collision, but not this time. The timing was so perfect that he took the full force of the wallop and I felt nothing.

Horton was looking at the puck as he tried to gain speed through neutral zone, and to me that was simply an invitation to be clobbered. Clearly, he never saw me coming and I buried my shoulder into him, probably head high. He was such a big strong horse that when he was lying there I began to wonder whether

I might have caught him with my elbow or the arm. The crowd was booing as loudly as I ever heard them boo in the Garden. The scare didn't leave me until Horton began to regain his senses. Even then it was evident he was in a lot of pain. We would find out later that he had suffered a broken jaw and leg on that play. My teammates told me later that they could see Horton's leg bend under him as he was going down from the force of my check. Referee Bill Chadwick was standing beside me, staring down at Horton. "I thought it was a pretty clean check, don't you think so?" I asked the veteran referee.

"You got nothing to worry about on that one," Chadwick said.

That made me feel better about my action. However the situation was far from defused. The crowd's hostility was growing, and fans in the front rows looked like they were ready to start forming a lynch mob. When I exited the ice after the period, Toronto general manager Connie Smythe was there waiting for in the runway and he was screaming and cursing like he had just been a witness to murder.

"I will have you suspended," he yelled at me. " I will have you kicked out of the league. You will never play again."

My response was equally profane, and I walked into the dressing room. Nothing ever came of Smythe's threats, and people still tell me that my wallop against Tim Horton was the hardest hit they've ever seen. When the Leafs moved out of Maple Leaf Garden, and they were revisiting some of the venue's memorable moments on Hockey Night in Canada, several ushers testified that my hit on Horton was the toughest bodycheck ever delivered in that shrine to hockey.

Truthfully, I enjoyed the physical side of hockey. I enjoyed hitting people with hard, clean bodychecks. I didn't want to maim my opponents, I just wanted to get their attention. My belief was that every time you hit someone you took something out of him. You might slow them down a half stride. You might make them hesitate to carry the puck at full speed toward your side of the ice. You might force them to worry a bit about where you were, and then that momentary loss of focus would cause them to miss a pass. Every time I decked an opponent, I believed it would payoff sometime down the road.

That was the way the game was played in those days. I certainly wasn't alone in my willingness to force opponents to keep their eyes forward and their head up as they were skating through toward our zone. Leo Boivin could really deliver a payload, as could the New York Rangers' Lou Fontinato and Detroit's Marcel Pronovost, and Jack Evans could really lay you out. It seems as if we had as many open-ice hits in one game as a team would have in a season today. Today's game doesn't foster the same level of animosity between opponents that we had. We played 70 games and there were only six teams. That meant we played each team 14 times and possibly another seven times in the playoffs. Grudges built up quickly, and lasted for longer periods of time. I played for the Chicago Blackhawks, New York Rangers and Detroit Red Wings during my career, and no matter where I played the principle of looking after your teammates was always the same. If a player cross-checked someone's face, there was no need for the league to suspend him because he would pay a far greater penalty by having to play against the same team sooner or later. If an opponent did something you didn't like in a road game, you might be playing him the next night in your arena. We played a lot of home and home series against each other, and if you didn't get even the next game, you could settle the score a week from then.

To appreciate what it was like in my era, you really have to watch New Jersey Devil's defenseman, Scott Stevens, play hockey today. He is a throwback to my era when your goal every game was to make your opponent feel some pain for not paying attention. Every playoff series Stevens is in, he makes two or three hits that leave the other team cursing and trying to shake the cobwebs out of their head.

If you saw the hit that Stevens laid on Eric Lindros a couple of years ago in the Eastern Conference Final, then you know how hard I hit Montreal Canadiens' winger Yvon Cournoyer in his rookie season. It was a very similar style of wallop. Cournoyer was cutting across the zone looking for the puck when I caught him high. Years after that hit, I ran into Phil Goyette who told me that the Canadiens all had some fun after that hit at Cournoyer's expense because Goyette had warned him to watch out for me before the game.

As Cournoyer, nicknamed the Roadrunner because of his speed, was lying on the bench trying to figure out who he was, Goyette leaned over him and said simply: "You idiot, I told you to watch out for No. 4." The players on the bench got a chuckle out of that, although I suppose Cournoyer probably didn't think it was very funny.

Today's players become upset when they are hit. In my era, it just came with the territory. If you let someone knock you silly, you felt two different kinds of pain. You experience the physical discomfort caused by the hit, and you felt embarrassed that you had put yourself into that position.

Although I thought it was better to give than receive, I took my fair share of hits. In 1948-49, Toronto's Bill Barilko hit me so hard at center ice that I was knocked out cold. I was 80% goofy even when I got to the bench, and it took a minute or two to regain my senses.

"That was like two freight trains colliding head-on," Chicago teammate Gus Bodnar yelled at me as I tried to figure out who I was, and why my head felt so fuzzy.

Actually I thought I was going to return to the game until I tried to move my left arm a little too much and I felt an excruciating pain in my shoulder. Blackhawks trainer Eddie Froelich guided me into the dressing room, and cut away my sweater. Imagine our surprise when we could see a shoulder separation that had broken right through the skin.

My teammates all told me it was a clean hit, and I figured that's what I deserved for having my head down.

That wasn't my only painful moment. In addition to the many broken noses, I broke my tibia in 1950-51, when Toronto's Cal Gardner jumped at me early in the season. Then I came back too early and separated the fracture on a leg-to-leg hit. I only played 25 games that season. Missing games wasn't my habit.

Two years later, I started a string in which I missed only seven games in six years. My belief was that if I had a pulse, I should play. In 1966, I played the Stanley Cup final with broken toes.

The most pain I ever experienced didn't involve

anything that happened on the ice. It involved a doctor trying to repair my face in the New York Rangers' dressing room. The injury occurred when a Chicago player took a big wind up on a slap shot. I blocked the puck, but the stick came up and sliced open my nostril. The skin above my nostril was flapping like a flag in the breeze and blood was everywhere.

When I got into the dressing room for stitches the Rangers' team doctor, Kazuo Yanagisawa, was waiting for me. He was a highly respected Japanese orthopedic surgeon and quite a colorful man. Built like a miniature sumo wrestler, Yanagisawa would wait down in the dressing room playing gin rummy. When a player was brought down into the room, Yanagisawa would simply put down his hand and begin stitching with the nonchalance of someone embroidering a pillowcase. As soon as he was done, he would go back to his game.

As he examined the injury, and reached for his needle, he gave me the kind of sympathetic look that told me that this was going to hurt me a lot more than it was going to hurt him.

"You had better hold onto the rubbing table because this is going to be painful," Yanagisawa said, and he wasn't lying. Most folks are surprised that we never received any Novocain or anything to numb the area that was being stitched. We were accustomed to a little pain, but this was more than I bargained for. That region of your nose is rather tender to say the least, and each time he would put a stitch in and lift it up to tie it up, I went right with him. If the table is in existence anywhere it has my hand prints permanently embedded in the edges that I dug into that table. That pain is still in my memory. It seemed like it took forever to stitch that wound, and when he was finished the game was over. Back then we used to park our car on Long Island and take the subway into the game, and I was quite a sight heading back home on the train.

A man sitting across from us looked on with amazement as my wound started to leak, and Edna was trying to get it under control with hankies, kleenex and everything else she could find. My face was a swollen purplish gob of blood and flesh.

Finally the man's curiosity must have overcome him because he asked us rather pointedly. "Were there fights at the Garden tonight?" he asked. "Are you are a fighter?"

I told him "Yea, Yea I'm a fighter." I was simply in too much pain to explain why I looked the way I did.

That fellow must have thought I took a whale of a beating in the ring. The next morning when Brenda got a look at her dad's face she uncorked a scream, my face was hideous.

That certainly wasn't the bloodiest injury I ever witnessed. Early in my career in Chicago my defensive partner was Ralph Nattrass from Saskatchewan. In one game he was backchecking and stumbled and fell on someone's skate. His cheekbone snapped, and the cut was so deep that the ice rapidly turned red. I have never seen so much blood. His face was black and blue the next day. It was the ugliest injury I ever saw.

That wasn't the most serious injury I ever saw. I was on the bench when Doug Barkley lost his eye while playing for the Detroit Red Wings. Doug Mohn's stick came up for just an instant and Barkley's career was over.

Hockey was a tough business, and no one thrived

in that environment more than Gordon Howe.
Even when we were adversaries early in my career,
Howe and I didn't hate each other. I always felt as if
there was a mutual respect because our approach was
similar. If you played it straight up with either one of
us, there was never any problem. You could hit Gordie
with a good, clean check and he never bothered you,
but if you cross-checked him in the back or got your
stick up, he would get you sooner or later. Gordie had a
memory like an elephant. He never forgot to settle a
score.

People talk about Wayne Gretzky, Mario
Lemieux and Bobby Orr maybe being the greatest
players of all time, but not one of those players was
better all-around than Gordie. I can guarantee you
that. I played with him, and I played against him. My
opinion never changed.

What I admired most about Gordie was that he
excelled at every aspect of the game. He was a tough
checker, a good penalty killer, he could make plays and
we all know he could score goals. He could shoot the
puck with either hand. And he came to play every
night.

Funny how people used to say that Gordie's
skating wasn't good enough. If he had the puck, and
there was one man to beat he always beat him. His
skating was fine.

Gordie never needed the referee to protect him,
and he didn't require an on-ice policeman to do his
dirty
work. No one ever had to look after Mr. Hockey.

One night in Montreal, the fans had given him a
huge ovation for reaching some milestone and five

minutes later they were booing him like he was Satan on skates. Nobody saw exactly what happened, but Gordie and Montreal's J.C. Tremblay went into the corner and a second later Tremblay dropped to the ice like a sack of potatoes. Gordie was assessed a five-minute major for intent to injure, and yet the referee didn't even know exactly what Gordie did. He probably just looked at Tremblay's crumpled form and assumed Gordie had done something outside the rulebook. This was a time when few games were televised, and there was no video replay available of every play. Plays happened so quickly that no one could be sure what had happened. You could slug someone and deny it afterward. When you tried to sort out what happened, everyone had a different version.

That's why I went over to my roommate Gordie to find out the truth of what happened in the corner between Tremblay and him

"What the hell did you do to Tremblay?" I asked my roommate. "I don't know what happened, Bill, just go play the game," Gordie said. After the game Gordie and I went out for a late supper, and I again asked Gordie to explain what had happened. "I really don't know, but maybe the thumb of my glove stuck him in the eye," Gordie said. "That's probably what happened."

That could happen, I told myself. That can really hurt. Satisfied that Gordie had given me the real scoop, we headed back to our room at Mount Royal Hotel. I wouldn't have given it another thought had I not picked up the Montreal newspaper before Gordie and I sat down for breakfast.

"Gordie, you must have some powerful thumb," I said, turning the paper around so he could view the headline. The headline screamed that Tremblay had suffered a broken jaw at the hands of Mr. Hockey.

As it turned out, Tremblay had crossed Gordie at some point before and he was merely settling that account. When Gordie cleared his ledger, pain was involved.

My hunch was that Tremblay had speared Gordie at some point, but when we were doing this book Gordie gave the real story.

The year before the Red Wings had been out of the playoffs Gordie had been working as a color analyst for radio for the Chicago-Montreal series. He was on a train between Chicago and Montreal watching a Canadiens' bridge game when he commented that Dick Duff had made a nice play.

Tremblay had turned to Gordie and said, "What's a dummy like you know about bridge?"

Gordie told Tremblay they would finish that discussion at some other time, and a year later Gordie made his point along the boards. He simply didn't forget to settle up.

In those days, players believed in frontier justice. Today, the NHL uses suspensions to deter players from committing acts of violence outside the rules of the game. In my era, players were dissuaded from those acts because they knew that at some future date they would have to answer for those acts on the ice with either the victim or the victim's teammate.

For example, I know Nick Knott, the opponent who cut me in his first minor league game, never made the NHL because I was looking for him. I wanted to settle our score.

In each of our heads was a mental score sheet on which we kept track of opponents who had wronged us, plus we had to remember who might be after us for what we might have done to them.

The notion of making an opponent pay for improper behavior was on my mind the night in the 1950s when I almost started a riot in Montreal because I felt obliged to attempt to chase Emile "Butch" Bouchard through the stands. The craziest element of this story is that Bouchard wasn't even playing that night.

The underlying cause of the mayhem was my fight with Montreal's Elmer Lach. In that scrap, I had pummeled Lach rather badly, and Bouchard had been watching angrily from the stands. He was a large strapping man, probably 6-foot-2, 215 pounds, and he always made it his job to make sure his teammates were protected. Apparently, he believed his obligation to perform his duties didn't stop when he wasn't wearing the sweater.

In those days, the penalty box was more or less located in the stands, and it was wide open. Any fan could reach in there, and that's what Bouchard did. Because I wasn't expecting anyone to blind-side me, he was able to march up to the box and cold-cock me to the jaw. The blow knocked me to the floor, and when I was able to regain my senses I was able to get up in time to see Bouchard heading up the stands. In the next temper-inspired moments, I was running on my skates up the stairs, stick in hand chasing Bouchard.

A few steps into my journey I was confronted by a short, stout police officer who seemed as wide as he was tall. Not giving any thought to the consequences, I speared the police officer right in the belly. Suddenly, there were police officers everywhere, blocking my path to Bouchard who had made good on his escape.

Witnessing this, several of my New York Rangers teammates had already entered the stands to come to my rescue. Cooler heads prevailed and the situation ended without further damage.

Presumably, I could have faced criminal charges for striking the police officer, but nothing ever came of it. League president, Clarence Campbell had once given a stern tongue lashing for shoving referee Frank Udvari, but he never called me about this episode.

The next time the Rangers were in Montreal, I sought out that police officer as soon as I arrived at the Forum. I apologized for my actions. "Bill," he said shaking my hand. "These things happen."

After that, every time I came to Montreal Forum that police officer was there to greet me with a smile and a handshake.

In those days, it seemed as if all of us had one opponent that served as our archenemy. Chicago Blackhawks, center Stan Mikita, was mine. Looking back, I probably hit him harder and more viciously than any player I ever faced. I knocked him cold a couple of times. As he was lying on the ice writhing in agony one time, I said to him, "one of these times you aren't going to get up."

That's how much I hated him. Sid Abel told me, one night at a bar, that when Mikita was skating down the ice toward me he could see my eyes get real big. I was like the tiger waiting for the gazelle to enter his hunting area.

Mikita, a fancy stickhandler, liked to try to stick the puck between your legs, and that meant his head would be down for just a fraction of a second. That's when I would flatten him.

In Mikita's first three or four years in the league he

might have been the dirtiest player in the league. If you were skating behind the net, he would be slashing your ankles or calves. He always carried his stick too high. He was mouthy. He acted like a jerk. There was a long line of players in the NHL who wanted to hurt Mikita.

My dislike of the man reached the point that Edna actually said to me, "Billy, you had better lay off Mikita or you are going to do something that you regret."

She was afraid that I might seriously hurt Mikita. To be honest, if Mikita wouldn't have changed his style of play he might not have lasted in the NHL. Guys hated him that much. He did change, to the point that late in his career he won the NHL's Lady Byng Award for gentlemanly play. In our retirement, he and I have talked casually, but never seriously discussed our feud.
Nothing needed to be said.

In 1988, when we were at the Salute to Excellence banquet, Mikita was making a speech and told the story of how he had appeared once on the cover of Sports Illustrated and he joked that I wouldn't let him show his face. I love that particular Sports Illustrated because it shows me with a headlock on Mikita. It's the Gadsby cover more than it is the Mikita cover. That picture of me tying up Mikita was symbolic of our feud.

In retrospect, as much as I despised Mikita there was a fire to him that I actually respected. This was an era when you had to be a warrior to play in the NHL, and he was that. One night I hit him with such force that he literally crawled to the bench, yet he was ready to go the next shift. Even when I hurt him, he came back for more. I admired his courage.

Within all of the rough play there was gamesmanship. Everyone would look for the big hit, and guys would try to set you up. In 1946-47, in my first trip to Boston, I remember seeing Milt Schmidt coming down the ice like he was the afternoon express. He was a powerful skater, and he could play prickly. In that era, the top players in the game, Rocket Richard, Schmidt, Gordie Howe and Ted Lindsay were as tough as they were talented. You knew you were dancing with a bobcat when you tried to tie them up, and you seldom caught these guys unaware in the open ice.

That's why my eyes lit up when I saw Schmidt with his head down. I nailed him with a solid check in the neutral zone and sent him tumbling. In the second period, he was coming toward me again and his head was down again. He looked like he wanted a second helping of what I could dish out and I was ready to serve it up. Just as I was about to explode into him, he leaped forward with both legs off the ice. I separated my chest bone, and missed two or three games. It was sore for a month.

Thirty years later Milt and I talked about that play and he remembered that particular play, and how he had set me up. "I saw you coming all the way," he said.

You didn't really hate an opponent in the Original Six, but you certainly weren't going to invite him over for Sunday dinner. When you happened to end up on the same train with an opposing team, you would walk through their car without saying a word.

You always had rivalries with certain players. Today Frank Mahovlich is a good friend, but when I played against him we were like the snake and the mongoose. Eleven minutes into the 1963 Stanley Cup final between my Red Wings and his Toronto Maple Leafs, I hit Mahovlich so hard that I thought both of us would be hospitalized. I was relatively surprised to find when I got off the ice that all our bones were in the alignment that God had intended. We hit knee against knee, and Mahovlich limped over to the bench.

Earlier that season, I had nailed Boston's Murray Oliver with the same kind of check and ended up getting penalized for kneeing. Oliver was out for five games. Maybe I deserved the penalty for the Oliver hit, but not the Mahovlich check. That was a fair hit. Mahovlich was a difficult man to catch because he always skated wide and then tried to tuck in behind you, but I guessed right when he was at top speed, and stepped into him.

When I was told after the game that Mahovlich was going to miss two or three games, my quote to the Toronto reporters was, "Too damn bad."

This story isn't presented to show how cold-hearted I was, it's presented to paint an honest picture of how competitive we were. We really didn't want to seriously hurt anyone, but our mind set was that if you could take someone out of a series with a clean check then you were doing your job. It was your opponent's job to avoid putting himself in that position. Guys who kept their head down were begging to be hit. Guys who tried to show you up were begging to be hit.

From my first NHL game with the Blackhawks in 1946-47 until my retirement from the Detroit Red Wings in 1965-66, I went into every game believing it would be a physical test. Each game was a battle, a physical confrontation between athletes who felt as if they had to prove they belonged in the NHL every day they were in it. To be honest, I liked the physical side of the sport. I liked that it required more than just athletic ability to be a successful player.

When I watch games on television today, and they marvel at players logging 28 minutes of ice time in a game, I chuckle. In my era, I was expected to play 33-34 minutes a game and I was disappointed when I didn't play that much. We carried five defensemen back then, and only four played a lot. Playing in the NHL during the Original Six era was like running the gauntlet. It was about surviving as much as it was winning.

Years after I retired, Montreal's managerial legend, Frank Selke, had put together a group of former Montreal Canadien players to tour European Military bases and play old-timers' games. Some big names were agreed to go, including Rocket Richard. He was short one defenseman, so I was invited, even though I had never played for the Canadiens. After one game, I was tired and went to bed early, and I must have been asleep a couple of hours when my roommate, Jimmy Peters, woke me up to tell me that Rocket Richard wanted me to come down to his room for a drink.

"Tell him I will have a drink with him tomorrow," I told Peters. "I'm tired tonight." Peters said Rocket wasn't going to like my rejection of his invitation. "Then tell him to come down and get me," I said, just wanting to be left alone.

A few minutes later there was a knock on the door, and when I opened it there stood Rocket Richard dressed only in his boxer shorts. He had the hairiest torso I had ever seen, and I was struck by how powerful he looked several years after he retired.

"Come down and drink some cognac with me," he said. Something told me I shouldn't turn down this invitation.

Once we got to his room, it was clear he just wanted to talk about old times when he and I were rival gladiators.

"Beeel," Rocket said, pronouncing my name with his thick French Canadian accent. "Every time I come down the ice, you take your stick and go chop-chop on my arm." He made a slashing motion on his wrist just to make sure I understood. "You stuck those arms out there, and I did what I had to do to slow you down," I said. "But after each of those games, my arms were blue-black," Richard said.

We both laughed. I remember that night well, and not just because Rocket didn't quite have the "black and blue" English phrase down pat. I remember it because it was a moment that two old rivals had acknowledged that each of them had done what they had to do in the name of winning, and there were no hard feelings.

That was simply how the game was played, and most of us were quite open about it. I remember that Toronto columnist Scott Young (father of famed rock and roller Neil Young) once wrote that what he admired most about me wasn't how well I played the game, but rather how honest I was in discussing the game.

Once Frank Mahovlich and I had a pretty healthy scrap after I pulled him down on a breakaway. When Mahovlich hit the ice, he was already swinging away at me. After the game Young asked me what happened, and one of my teammates jumped in and started ranting about how Mahovlich had been the dirty player because he had been slugging me without provocation. Finally, when my long-winded teammate had run out of verbiage or breath, I turned to Young and said, "I high-sticked Mahovlich. That's what happened."

When the late Carl Brewer was playing for Toronto, he and I ended up behind the Toronto net with our sticks up much higher than they should have been. Again Young asked me to explain what had transpired to cause such a ruckus. "I hit him in the head with my stick," I said. "And I guess he didn't like it." Then I smiled and said, "I've been hit in the head with a stick from time to time myself, and I didn't much like it either."

When my close friend Gordie Howe retired from hockey he had played 32 seasons and collected 1,071 goals. That's an average of 31 goals per season. When I retired from hockey after 20 seasons I had collected 640 stitches. That's an average of 32 stitches per season. Both of us are equally proud of our numbers.

"Oh Mighty Hunter"
Bill Gadsby circa
1945-46

Bill Gadsby & Edna
Anfindsen 1947

Bill & Edna Gadsby
Banff, Alberta Honey-
moon 1952

Lars Anfindsen, Bill's
father-in-law and fishing
buddy Lake Wabamun
1960

Wedding Day June 16, 1952
William & Elizabeth Gadsby (center) Bill & Edna
Gadsby, Lars and Bertha Anfindsen
Edmonton, Alberta Canada

Wedding Party (best man) Cy Thomas (ushers) Clarence
Moher and Neil Moher (maid of honor) Maragaret
Anfindsen (bridesmade) Maxine MacDonald

Bill & the guys

Brenda's Christening 1953 3-1/2
Months old

Bill with Brenda 5 months
old Chicago 1953

Gordie Howe & Bill 1954

Bill, Brenda and Judy
New York 1957

Letter from Bill to his sweetheart, Edna in 1945

Letter from Bill to Edna while in hospital with Polio

Letter from Bill to his 4 month old daughter, Brenda

1939 England,
Visiting Relatives

1949 Calgary, Alberta
Visiting Mr. & Mrs. Gadsby

My home in Calgary where I grew up - flowers everywhere!

1956, Brenda fishing with Dad - Seba Beach, Alberta

1957, Taking Brenda & Judy to Rockefeller Center, New York

1958, Banff, Alberta Bill with Brenda and Judy

Fun on skates:
Dearborn Michigan
1962 - Judy, Donna
and Sandy with Mom

1963 - Detroit Red
Wings Christmas Party.
Sandy With Santa
(Sonny Elliot)

At our cottage Lake
Wabamun, Alberta
1966

Bill with Judy, Donna &
Sandy - our cottage Lake
Wabamun, Alberta 1967

"Timmy, Tam & Tot" The
dump family of kittens with
Bill at Lake Wabamun,
Alberta 1968

Hunting in Alberta

Fishing in Panama
Marty Howe, Gordie
Howe, and John
Curran in the '60s

1967 - Fishing
in Florida

Gordie and I with
our fishing guide
in Ecuador

The Howe's & Gadsby's
on Vacation, Florida
1965

June 1977 in Houston Texas, Marty & Mary Howe's wedding

June 1977 Honolulu, Hawaii - with Cathy & Colleen Howe

Kona - Hawaii 1977

25th Wedding Anniversary, June 16, 1977 Maui, Hawaii

Judy & Ron's Wedding-Northbrook Presbyterian
Beverly Hills, MI. June 28, 1975

Brenda & Dennis's Wedding-Northbrook
Presbyterian Beverly Hills, MI. April 29, 1977

Donna & Mark's Wedding - Northbrook Presbyterian Beverly Hills, MI. May 16, 1981

Sandy & Ed's Wedding - Northbrook Presbyterian
Beverly Hills, MI. February 19, 1983

June 28, 1975 - Judy & Ron's Wedding, Bill with his mother, brother Harold & his wife Hazel

Edna's parents Lars and Bertha with Colleen Howe

July 1979 -
Our first grandchild
Mark Golembiewski

Grandpa Bill with Gina - 1981
our second grandchild

Grandpa Bill builds a
snowman for Gina & Mark

Grandpa Bill visits
grandsons Travis
and Garet Malott at
their school 1990

At Bill Gadsby's Hockey
School with son-in-law Mark
and grandson Travis 1984

At Bill Gadsby's Hockey
School with grandsons Billy,
Lance, Travis, Alex, and Garet

Grandson James on the
tractor with Grandpa Bill

Grandsons Lance, Billy & Michael summer 1985

Feb. 1989 - Lac St. Anne Alberta - Lorne and
Anne Anfindsens home Loranwood

Edna's sister Margaret, husband Con Richens' & their
family 2000. Edmonton, Alberta

Fishing with friend Greg Papp early 90's

Fishing with the late Al Philpott, Miami 1990

Florida early 90's with Don Sudnik

Feeding the pigeons
Trafalgar Square, London,
England 1992

London, England 1992
- great trip with Lorne
& Anne

Lillehammer, Norway
1992

Chateau Lake Louise, Alberta 1989 - with Edna's
brother Lorne

A trip back home 1995 - Bow Falls, Banff, Alberta -
where I proposed to Edna in 1951

June 1992 - taken for our 40th wedding anniversary, Brenda, Judy, Donna, Sandy. The "fab 4"

Feb. 1991 - at the "Joe" with grandpa - James, Billy, Gina, Travis, and Garet

Easter Sunday 1989 with our nine grandchildren

With former team-
mate and friend
Jimmy Peters

The Stanley Cup Party at Dr.
Finley's with son-in-law Mark
Malott

Golfing with son-in-law Ron Rinderknecht

Our nine grand-
children taken
July 1988

Grandparents Day at
school with Alex 1998

Our super
son-in-laws
Ed Groth, Mark
Malott and Ron
Rinderknecht
1999

Calgary, Alberta -
"Salute to Excel-
lence" 1989 with
Eddie Shack, Boom
Boom Geoffrion,
& Gordie

A visit with former
New York Ranger
teammates -
Andy Bathgate,
Harry Howell at
Lou Fontinatos
farm late 80's

In Chicago
Sept. 2002 with
Mr. Hockey® &
The Great One

A corner of my
office at home

Induction into
Alberta Sports Hall
of Fame - Red
Deer, Alberta 1986

Opening of new Hall of Fame in Toronto former
teammates Norm Ullman & Frank Mahovlich 1993

Maui friends
Patty &
George
Klempert
Maui 1999

Our close
friends Maxine
& Ray Goss
Louise Allen,
Edmonton
Alberta Sept.
2001

Our close friends
Shirley & Frank
Bassen former Red
Wings teammate -
Calgary Alberta Sept.
2001

Christmas with Colleen & Gordie - 2000

Jasper Park Lodge Alberta with Edna's
brother Lorne and wife Anne 2001

In our beloved Maui with dear friends Maxine and Ray
Goss winter 2002

Dear friends Bill and May Pringle from Calgary,
Alberta in Maui Hawaii

Taken June 16, 2002 our 50th Wedding Anniversary at
the Whitney, Detroit

June 16, 2002 with our nine grandchildren

June 16, 2002 with dear friends Jack & Genevieve Finley

June 16, 2002 dear friends Joe & Val Gagnon

Our grandchildren taken June 16, 2002, our 50th
Wedding Anniversary

Our family taken June 16, 2002 our 50th
Wedding Anniversary

The Howe and Gadsby family vacation Homosassa, Florida with Clarence the cross-eyed Lion 1969

Doing an orange juice commercial in Florida in the 60's

Colleen and Edna Christmas 2000

Bill, Kevin, Mike & Edna working on the book 2002

Chapter 7

News of my trade from the New York Rangers to the Detroit Red Wings February 5, 1960, was delivered by the toughest messenger boy I had ever encountered.

Gordie Howe gave me the word as I was trying to jam him rudely into the boards.

"Hey, lighten up," Howe said. "You are coming here tomorrow in the trade."

As much as I trusted Gordie, it was still difficult to believe him. As a player you learn to be skeptical about trade rumors or whispers. In the weeks before being traded from the Chicago Blackhawks to the New York Rangers in 1954, rumors had me being dealt to the Toronto Maple Leafs. None had me going to New York.

"Gordie, you big palooka, you had better not be joking with me," I told him as I held him along the boards.

"It's true you are coming here," Gordie said. "So lighten up, because you are beating us 3-2."

As Gordie skated away, I yelled, "yea and I'm going to keep beating you the rest of the night."

That was my competitiveness talking, but I was thrilled at the thought of being a Detroit Red Wings player. Even when I was with the Chicago Blackhawks, Sid Abel used to tell me that if he returned to Detroit he was going to try to trade for me. That idea appealed to Edna and me for a couple of reasons. First the Red Wings were a talent-laden club and our friend Gordie Howe was on that squad. Secondly, the Red Wings minor league affiliate was in Edmonton and in the back of our minds we kept thinking that after I retired I could end up either coaching or working for the Edmonton Flyers. To us that seemed like the best way to go home and stay in hockey.

Once I was dealt to the New York Rangers, Abel apparently had tried, on a few occasions, to acquire my rights but the Rangers weren't interested in trading me. Abel made it clear he still wanted me because each time he came to Madison Square Garden with the team, he would see me before the game and ask, "You still interested in coming to Detroit?" When I would tell him that would make me very happy, he would say that he would see what he could do.

As it turned out, Gordie knew what he was talking about. That didn't surprise me because Sid and Gordie were extremely good friends and Sid probably told Gordie exactly what was going on.

After the game as I was walking off the ice, Rangers general manager, Muzz Patrick, was there to tell me that he had traded Eddie Shack and me to Detroit for Red Kelly and Billy McNeill, who was from Edmonton. The deal was announced to the media after the game, and since Kelly and I were both All-Star caliber players, it created quite a stir. I was 32 at the time, and only one season removed from one of my best offensive seasons. In 1959-60, I registered 46 assists to erase Doug

Harvey's record of 44 assists by a defenseman, set two seasons before.

Obviously I was ecstatic about the deal because it appeared that our own personal master plan was working out perfectly. I immediately called Edna and told her I would be staying in Detroit, which meant that she would have to pack up everything once again all by herself. Some of the Rangers' wives came over. Doreen Worsley, Merle Bathgate and Harry Howell's wife, Marilyn came too. It was quite a gang and they worked until 3:30 in the morning to get Edna ready to drive to Detroit.

The fact that Edna was ready to go in just a few hours is more incredible when you consider that she also had to find homes for three or four kittens.

Brenda came home from school one day and said a stray cat had followed her home, although we were reasonably sure that she had coaxed it home. She begged us to allow her to keep her new feline friend, and we did, even though we saw right away the cat was pregnant. She had given birth to her kittens not long before the trade was announced, which simply complicated Edna's moving preparations.

Today's athletes make enough money that they just move to the next town and worry about the previous home later on. However, back then security deposits, transportation and moving costs were important economic issues to us. Even though we were only in Edmonton six months out of the year, we considered that our home and we rented everywhere else. Finding a suitable rental house every fall was a major aggravation.

While Edna was busy re-arranging our life, I was back in the Rangers' dressing room listening to Shack

getting ready to launch verbal fireworks over this trade.
He was also thrilled by the trade, but for a different
reason. I had nothing against the Rangers, and I
enjoyed my time there. Eddie, The Entertainer Shack,
didn't enjoy his stay in New York.

As I was watching Eddie talk to our teammates, I
suddenly got the feeling that something could go wrong
with the trade. Out of nowhere it began to occur to me
that Red Kelly might balk at this trade. He had been in
Detroit many years, and maybe he wouldn't go.
Before the reporters came in, I turned to Eddie and
said, "Hey Eddie, I know you don't like New York, the
management and the fans, but you had better close it up
on these interviews tonight because this trade could fall
apart, and maybe Red Kelly won't go."

Eddie heard me, but he didn't seem to care. You
would think that someone nicknamed The Entertainer
would have enjoyed the Big Apple, but Shack was bitter
about his New York experiences. Much of Eddie's
dissatisfaction was derived from head butting with the
late Phil Watson who had been the New York Rangers
coach from 1955-1960.

To be honest, Phil wasn't my favorite coach,
either. He knew what he was doing as a coach, but he
didn't know how to deal with people. It just seemed as
if he went out of his way to annoy the players. Edna
and I remember the night he called my house at 11 p.m.
to see if I was home. Essentially, he was doing a curfew
check on a player who had been in the league for ten
years and had three children at home.

When I picked up the phone and realized it was
Watson, I told him what I thought about his
bed-checks. "You just woke up my kids and I think you
should come over and get them back to sleep," I said.

"Don't ever call me at home this late again."

Watson could be downright mean. If he wasn't happy with your play, he would belittle you in the newspaper. Guys didn't like that at all. One time, Watson was unhappy with Gump Worsley's play in goal, and he told reporters that Gump's difficulty resulted from him having a "beer belly." The next day Gump came in and told our non-beloved coach that he had mis-spoken in his comments to the press the night before.

"I don't even drink beer," Gump said. "I only drink VO (whiskey)."

Gump had a few other well-chosen words for Watson as well, and I remember thinking that I would wake up the next day and hear that Gump had been sent to our minor-league team in Springfield.

As it turned out Watson didn't demote Gump, but I bet he considered it. Watson liked to bully players, and he routinely used the threat of minor league demotion.

Watson had favorite targets for his abuse. For example, he always rode defenseman Larry Cahan particularly hard about his weight. He would weigh him constantly and tell him that if he didn't make a specific goal he would send him to the minors.

As we sat together next to each other one day, Larry confided in me that he hadn't eaten anything but one chocolate bar for a couple of days. "Even if Watson puts me in the lineup, I don't know if I can play. I'm that weak," Cahan told me. Shortly thereafter Larry had his head down, and said to me in a low voice, "Is Watson looking this way?" When I told him that Watson wasn't looking, he pulled a candy bar from down by his skates, unwrapped it in a quick motion and stuffed it in his mouth and began chewing, trying to be inconspicuous in case Watson should reappear.

Watson always wanted to intimidate players. Young players, and players on the bubble, worried every day that their jobs were in jeopardy. Watson never let you forget that he had the power to alter your life.

Years after we were all retired, I remember Cahan telling me that he saw Watson at a public gathering and he had tried to get his attention, but Cahan pretended he didn't see him. Time hadn't healed the wounds as far as he was concerned.

Shack and Watson were like two rams battering their horns against each other on a regular basis. Watson didn't seem to like Shack much, and the feeling was mutual. Watson didn't play Shack very often. One day in practice, Watson was making some point and asked whether Shack had understood. Eddie took his two fingers and motioned as if he was pushing Watson's words into his ear, and then he took his fingers and made a motion as if the words were going out the other ear. The next day Watson demoted Shack to Springfield.

The funny thing is that Watson was already gone by the time the Rangers had traded the two of us to the Red Wings. He had been fired and replaced by Alfie Pike a month before, but there was too much bad karma for Shack in New York and he still wanted out.

When the photographers came in and the reporters had their notebooks out, Shack lashed out at everything and everyone connected with New York. Imagine the horror on his face when Pike approached us at breakfast the next morning to tell us that the trade was off because Kelly wouldn't report. Shack turned to me, and said, " What are you, some kind of psychic?"

As it turned out, McNeil refused to report as well, because he had lost his wife to polio and he was trying to raise his children by himself. He had his childcare set up in Detroit, and he didn't know anyone in New York.

Now imagine Edna's shock when I informed her that we were staying in New York. Having written letters to everyone saying we were leaving, Edna had to sit down and write new letters to say we were staying.

NHL Commissioner, Clarence Campbell, put the trade on hold for 48 hours, while everyone tried to talk Kelly into reporting, but he had family issues of his own, and wouldn't budge. On February 7, Campbell officially nullified the trade.

Having popped off to the media, Shack was even more uncomfortable in a Rangers jersey than he was before. He lasted through the end of that season in New York, but at the start of the following season he was dealt to Toronto for Pat Hannigan and Johnny Wilson, the latter now being a good friend of mine.

Sixteen months later, with considerable less fanfare, I was traded in the off season for $20,000 and Les Hunt, a prospect who never made it to the NHL.

What makes this story interesting to me is that today most fans associate me with the Red Wings. Truth is, I only played five seasons with the Red Wings. That's only 25% of my of my 20-season playing career. Compare that to the parts of nine seasons I played with the Chicago Blackhawks or parts of seven seasons I played with the New York Rangers.

Maybe I'm associated with the Red Wings because I've lived in Michigan 33 years. Probably some fans think of me as a Red Wing player because the majority of my playoff experience came wearing the winged wheel on my chest. In my long career, I played only 67 playoff games, and 40 of those were with the Red Wings. Three times we reached the Stanley Cup Final and each time we were stymied in the championship series.

It's fair to say that I was re-energized by this trade to Detroit, because I was going to an exceptional team and the management of that team believed I would be vital to their championship hopes. After years of just hoping I could be on a championship team, I really believed I had a very good shot with the Red Wings.

When I came to the Red Wings at age 34, I was still playing some of the best hockey of my career. Five years before, as a defenseman, I tied for ninth in the NHL scoring race with 51 points and I had matched that point total in 1958-59 when I broke Harvey's assist record. The season before I came to Detroit, I netted nine goals, but really I thought I was playing better than ever defensively. My defensive game had evolved dramatically since the day I showed up in Chicago looking to make a name for myself with some big hits and big goals.

In my first few seasons, I did a lot of running around, looking for board checks and big hits. In my fourth NHL season, I totaled 138 penalty minutes, and Charley Conacher, who had succeeded Johnny Gottselig as coach, came in and straightened me out. Since I could carry the puck pretty well, he reminded me that I was more valuable to my team on the ice than off the ice.

When Ebbie Goodfellow succeeded Conacher, he taught me the art of eliminating a player from the play without drawing a penalty. He taught me how to force a player to go wide so he would have no shooting angle, and on my own, I figured out how to block shots without getting myself maimed in the process. By the time I got to Detroit I would like to believe that I had my position figured out as well as anybody else in the league.

Was I frustrated with my lack of post season success? Sure I was, but I didn't dwell on it because I knew that I was doing all that I could.

People have said I played for some bad clubs in my career, but it always seemed like we had enough talent to compete. When I arrived in Chicago the Blackhawks boasted Max and Doug Bentley who were two of the NHL's most skilled forwards. Because Red Wings owner, Bruce Norris, and Chicago owner, Jim Norris, were brothers, they were always trying to help each other be successful, but it never seemed to work out.

When the Blackhawks traded Max Bentley and my close friend Cy Thomas (he was best man at my wedding) for Bud Poile, Gus Bodnar, Gaye Stewart, Ernie Dickens and Bob Goldham on November 2, 1947, I thought Chicago president, Bill Tobin, had made a great deal. Goldham was one of the best shot blockers in NHL history, and all five of those players were quality athletes, but that just didn't put us over the top. We always seemed to be a player or two short of getting the job done.

It did seem as if we were snake bit at times, particularly in 1952-53, when I was playing for the Blackhawks and we had a 3-2 lead in the best-of-seven semifinals against Montreal. We thought we were in control because Gerry McNeil appeared shaky in goal.

They surprised us by opting to use a rookie goaltender in Game 6. We were surprised again when the rookie posted a shutout in Game 6. The rookie who beat us was this unheralded prospect named Jacques Plante. Re-energized by the win in Game 6, the Canadiens beat us in Game 7 in Montreal.

In 1957-58, I qualified for the playoffs with the New York Rangers. We owned a 1-0 lead against Boston, and were up by a goal with ten minutes left in Game 2. The bad playoff luck struck me again. I suffered a shoulder separation and was forced to leave the game. The Bruins tied the game, and won on Jerry Toppazzini's overtime goal. Even though I played with the injury, I was probably playing at 60% efficiency at best, and we lost the series.

The following season we lost fourth place (the final playoff spot) to the Toronto Maple Leafs on the final night of the regular-season. Lady Luck never seemed to be in my line-up.

That's why I was overjoyed to come to the Motor City where there was a strong tradition of NHL playoff success.

They had reached the Stanley Cup Final five times in the 1950s, and won four championships. There was no question in my mind that the Red Wings had enough talent to win two or three Cups before I retired. Imagine my surprise when we didn't win any. We reached the Stanley Cup Final in 1962-63, 1963-64 and 1965-66, and I left each time without a ring. We finished first overall in 1964-65 only to be upset by the Chicago Blackhawks in the first round. We held a 3-2 lead in that series, and then lost Game 6 in Chicago and Game 7 in Detroit.

When I look back at those teams I really wonder

how in the world we didn't win a title. Gordie Howe
was on that squad, as was Alex Delvecchio. Parker
McDonald was a 30-goal scorer in 1962-63, and Norm
Ullman was a terrific player. He doesn't get enough
credit for the kind of player he was. He was a very
quiet man who let his play do his talking. The Red
Wings goaltender, when I got there, was Terry
Sawchuk, who is clearly one of the greatest goaltenders
in NHL history.

A book about Sawchuk written by David Dupuis
(Sawchuk: The Troubles and Triumphs of the World's
greatest Goalie) in 1998 painted a disturbing picture of
the man we called "Ukey". Most of us who played with
him didn't know how violent he was at home. We knew
he didn't like being around people all the time. We
knew he didn't enjoy having the media around. We
certainly knew he was moody. After joining the Red
Wings, I ended up being Sawchuk's roommate for a
while and I would get up and say "Good morning,
Ukey." He wouldn't say a word.

Had I ticked him off? Was there something
wrong with Sawchuk? When I expressed my concern to
Gordie, he just told me, "Don't worry about it. That's
just the way he is."

One of my favorite Sawchuk stories involves a
fishing trip several of us took to the Florida Keys in the
summer of 1962. Marcel Pronovost was on the trip,
along with Gordie, coach Sid Abel and myself. It was a
great trip. Gordie snagged a sail fish and I brought in a
barracuda, and I remember Sawchuk hooked a Benito
tuna. It probably took him the better part of an hour to
reel in that fish, but he was having a grand time. We all
were, however the seas were rough, and the boat began
rising and falling like we were on a carnival ride. That

didn't bother anyone except Sawchuk. He looked like he wanted to be anywhere except on that boat. He became seasick and was throwing up every few minutes. His stomach finally seemed to calm down enough so he could sit down at the table in the galley, but he still looked awful.

The problem was that it was lunch time and I was in charge of getting that together and without giving it any thought I opened up a jar of dill pickles and the garlic aroma quickly filled the cabin. Sawchuk looked at me as if I had opened a canister of lethal cyanide gas.

"You did that on purpose," he screamed as he hurried up on deck to begin another round of vomiting.

Of course I hadn't done it on purpose, but he never let me forget that day. He brought it up every chance he could after that.

Although we all had days when Terry may have irritated us, there was no denying his ability to play between the pipes. I was very impressed with Sawchuk when I played against him, and even though I was recognized as an All-Star by the time I came to Detroit, I listened when Terry talked to defenseman about how he wanted us to play in front of him. Shortly after I arrived in Detroit, he pulled me aside and I talked about my shot blocking prowess and he asked me to keep my legs closed when I blocked shots because it was easier for him to see shots ripping past the outside of my legs than it was to see shots squeezing through my pads.

He knew his craft. Sometimes it's forgotten that the night Gordie scored his 545th goal to pass Rocket Richard and become the NHL's all-time leading goal scorer, Sawchuk made 39 saves to record his 94th shutout to tie George Hainesworth's NHL record for career shutouts. That record was supposed to be among the league's safest.

The Red Wings had other memorable characters in that era, none more colorful than Howie Young. He toiled for the Red Wings from 1960-61 to 1962-63 and then again from 1966-67 to 1967-68 and lived up to his nickname of "Wild Thing." No one else in the world could say he shared the stage with both Gordie Howe and Frank Sinatra. He wasn't a great hockey player, but he wasn't shy on the ice. In 1962-63, he established an NHL record of 273 penalty minutes that lasted until 1970-71. When he wasn't creating a ruckus in the NHL, he fancied himself an aspiring actor and actually landed a role as one of the marines in the 1966 classic, "None But the Brave", starring Sinatra and Clint Walker.

While much of Sawchuk's self destructive behavior was done behind closed doors, Howie's wildness was known to all of us. Drinking often landed Young in trouble.

In a futile effort to reform Young, Abel decreed that Gordie Howe, Alex Delvecchio and I each had a turn as his roommate. The idea, was we would counsel Young, keep track of his whereabouts and provide an example of how players should conduct themselves off the ice. We all tried to embrace this mentoring program, but it didn't seem to make much of an impact. He still would wander in at 3 a.m. even on our watch.

One night, when we were home, I got a call from Sid asking me if I would go to a bar on West Chicago and try to convince Young to go home. A waitress had called to say that Young was drunk and belligerent, and they wanted him out of there. When I arrived I found Howie at a payphone. He was doing a poor job of trying to converse with someone while rolling his own cigarette. Even though it was a serious situation, it was a comical sight because he was trying to lick the paper and his tongue never came within six inches of the paper. In his drunken state, his depth perception was non-existent.

Expecting Howie would resist my efforts to convince him to go home, I tried to swipe his keys from him before he knew what was going on. Words weren't getting anywhere with him, and he suddenly bolted out of the bar and got into his car. Quickly he was just flying down West Chicago with me following behind as fast as the law would allow. Unlike Howie, I was stopping at the red lights.

His home wasn't far from the tavern, and I was pulling up in front just as Howie was stumbling up the stairs. I was trying to intercept Howie before he got to the door. I had just hit the stairs when the porch light blinked on and Young's wife was standing in the doorway. An argument quickly started and before I could react Howie had swung at his wife. That was too much for me to take. I backhanded Young and knocked him off the porch. Young was incoherent when I picked him up off the lawn, and ushered him into his house.

Arriving at practice the next day, I suspected that Young might confront me about the incident. The thought crossed my mind that he might take a swing at me, particularly when he showed up with his face looking as if he had been pummeled by a two-by-four. His eye looked hideous; the eye socket swollen and discolored by my blow.

Imagine my alarm when he came straight to me in the dressing room and all he said was, "I must have had quite a night last night because I have no idea how I got this," pointing to his tender eye.

Needless to say I didn't feel that was the time to tell him exactly what had happened to him the night before.

It was never news when Hughie (that's what I always called him) was in trouble, nor was it rare for him to be upset by various issues of every day living. That's why I was trying to ignore him one payday when he was ranting about the puniness of his take-home pay.

"Look at my check, Bill. How do they expect me to live on this?" he said.

"I don't want to see your check, Hughie," I said. "That's your business."

"No, Bill look at this," he insisted.

Realizing he was never going to shut up, I looked at the check he was pushing in front of my face. I was aghast. His net pay was $9.54.

All the rest of his money had gone to league fines for misconducts, and team fines and other claims that various folks had against his money.

"How can I live on this?" Young repeated.

At that moment I felt sorry for Young. He played more than ten years in the NHL, and another decade in various leagues, including the World Hockey Association. Throughout his career those who knew him worried about him, but he wasn't the kind of man who reacted well to others telling him how to live.

At age 48, he tried to make a comeback with the Flint Generals in the International Hockey League in 1985. Maybe he needed the money, but it only lasted a few games.

In 1999, former teammates told me that Young wasn't doing well, and I called him. We talked for a few

minutes about old times, and then emotions got the best
of Young and he couldn't finish the conversation. Two
or three weeks later I received word that he had died. It
made me sad because Hughie always seemed like a man
who was just trying to find his place. When I think of
Howie Young, I try to remember the good times.

We had a lot of fun in those days with the Red
Wings, particularly at practices. We had our share of
pranksters. More than once you might go outside on a
chilly day to discover your car wouldn't start because a
teammate had unattached your battery cables. Floyd
Smith was a prankster, and so was Roger Crozier and
my good-friend Hank Bassen who was a back-up
goaltender. One of my favorite pranks was nailing
Hank's shoes to the floor one day at practice. We were
a close knit bunch of guys, and sometimes we acted like
kids on the playground. When we were in a playful
mood, nothing seemed too childish for us.

Maybe we needed that as a release because we
were so serious about our hockey. In the 1960s, the Red
Wings were serious about trying to restore the roar they
had in the 1950s.

In hindsight, the loss in the 1964 championship
series against Toronto bothered me more than any other
series I ever lost, because we had a 3-2 lead in that
best-of-seven series and Game 6 was in Detroit.

We were the underdogs going into that series
because the Maple Leafs had claimed 19 out of a
possible 28 points in our 14 regular-season meeting. To
make matters worse, Sawchuk injured his shoulder in
the first round against Chicago and wasn't close to
being 100% healthy going into the Final.

When Alex Delvecchio beat goaltender Johnny
Bower with 17 seconds remaining to give the Red Wings

a 4-3 win in Game 3, we felt as if we were a team on a mission. The fans sensed our confidence, and the Red Wings packed Olympia for Game 4, plus sold almost 5,000 tickets for fans to watch the game on a movie screen at Woods and Palms Theaters. The town was buzzing about the Red Wings. We lost that Game 4, but Sawchuk was unbelievable in Game 5 as we beat the Leafs 2-1 to put me one game away from winning my first championship.

That 1963-64 edition of the Red Wings was a nice blend of youth and experience. Meshing with veterans like Howe, Delvecchio and Sawchuk, we had youngsters like Pit Martin and Paul Henderson. We were so focused on trying to win that championship that coach Sid Abel decided we'd have the team stay 60 miles away in Toledo for the playoffs to avoid distractions.

What I remember about that series was that Gordie and I were so keyed up we couldn't even eat before the playoff games. At the pre-game meal, the youngsters like Martin and Henderson would be wolfing down steaks and Gordie and I would be dining on eggs and toast. Our stomach just couldn't take a heavy meal before an important game.

I wanted that championship so badly that Abel said in the paper he thought Gadsby would probably swallow a puck whole if it helped us win. What we didn't know when we forged that 3-2 lead is that the series that looked like it belonged to us, actually would belong to defenseman Bobby Baun for all eternity. That's the playoff series that gets the most notoriety because that's the year Baun supposedly played on a broken leg in Game 6 of the Final. I say supposedly because every time I see him, I jokingly told him that I

still don't think the leg was broke. Maybe he had a
hairline crack in his bone, but it wasn't any
compound fracture. He's gotten a lot of ink with that
story. What nobody remembers is that less than a
minute before Baun fired the shot that made him
famous, I took a shot that haunts me to this day.
Rushing into the Toronto zone with the puck, I spotted
right wing Floyd Smith. As soon as I sent him the puck,
he knew that I was going to be moving into the high slot
for the return feed. We had worked on that give-and-go
hundreds of times in practice. Just as planned, the
puck was feathered nicely toward me and I sent what
appeared to be the perfect one-timer over goaltender
Johnny Bowers shoulder. The play developed so quickly
and efficiently that Bower never even reacted to the
shot. The play was so perfect that I was already raising
my stick to celebrate as the puck was about to whiz past
Bower. Then history changed. Instead of finding the
net, the puck found the shaft of Bowers stick and
caromed harmlessly over the net. Stunned as I was, my
instincts carried me back toward my own zone in a
hurry. When Baun entered the zone with the puck, I
was at my defensive post. I was between Baun and the
net. When Baun unleashed his shot, it fluttered toward
the net like a Hoyt Wilhelm knuckleball.

That season was my 18th in the league, and I
probably had blocked a few thousand shots in my
career. Many of those shots had been scary blasts that
came at me with a force of a cannon. How ironic that a
puck that looked as harmless as a butterfly would cause
me so much pain.

Bauns shot struck my stick, and the puck
caromed up, just missing my head, and danced over
Sawchuk to give the Maple Leafs a 4-3 overtime victory.

In hindsight I wished that shot would have hit me square in the bean. Given all the stitches that had been sewn into my face by that time, what would a few more mattered? As Abel had said, I would have gladly swallowed that puck.

Everyone remembers the Game 6 dramatics, and forgets that Toronto beat us 4-0 in Game 7. That game also bothers me. Detroit Free Press hockey columnist, Jack Berry, wrote afterward that I had been the standout performer in the post-season because of how aggressively I had played. It seemed as if I had blocked a season's worth of shots in that Toronto series. Abel called me a master of the game. That did little to ease the frustration of losing those final two games to the Maple Leafs.

While the 1964 loss bothers me the most, many point to the 1966 Final as the one that should cause me the most frustration. Before the 1964-65 season, Abel made a difficult decision of dropping Sawchuk as our goaltender in favor of Crozier, considered to be a rising young star. Abel allowed Sawchuk to go to the Maple Leafs for the $20,000 waiver price. Abel would joke later that even his daughter, Linda, questioned his sanity about that move. Some folks thought that was a mistake, but I can tell you that naming Roger Crozier as our starting goaltender wasn't a step down. Sawchuk was a Hall of Fame goaltender, but he was in the twilight of his career. Crozier was a youngster on his way up. Crozier was a contortionist. He was twisting his body like a pretzel and kicking up his legs and arms before Dominik Hasek was born.

Crozier, who died in 1999, could make some amazing saves. If he wasn't bothered so much by illness in his career he would have been recognized as one of the best.

With Crozier in our nets, we had the league's best record (40-23-7) in 1964-65, but we were upset by Chicago in the seven-game playoff semifinal. The 1965-66 season was a different story because we reached the final and really believed we had a chance to win, even though the Canadiens had finished the season first overall.

When the 1965-66 season began, I was 38 and had been pondering retirement for a couple of seasons, but I certainly wasn't completely sold on the idea. Perhaps as an accommodation to age and the presence of puck-carrying Doug Barkley, my style had changed over the two previous seasons. I was staying home more and concentrating more on the defensive game, but a good player knows when he is playing well and when he isn't and I was still playing well enough to be a top two defenseman at the NHL level, but I also knew that at the end of the previous two seasons, I could tell my body was worn down.

Edna always said that the decision to retire had to be my own, because only I knew how I felt mentally and physically. Her only request was that I would promise to tell her first when I was ready to hang my skates on the nail. She didn't want to read it in the newspaper, or hear it on the radio. She wanted me to tell her when I was ready to quit. She knew that playing 20 years was important to me, and she also knew that I shared her desire to live year-round in Edmonton.

One shocking development had certainly worked against our retirement plan because the Edmonton Flyers franchise had folded, leaving me no place to work in hockey in Edmonton, or so I thought. Around

Christmas time Wild Bill Hunter, who owned the
Edmonton Oil Kings junior team, had talked to me
about coaching his team the following season. I told
him I was thinking about playing another season or
two, but would get back to him. Hunter was quite a
character, the smoothest operator I ever met. This guy
could sell palm trees in Alaska. He was the P.T.
Barnum of hockey, but I just didn't know if that's what
I wanted to do, nor did I know if I was ready to quit.

The Red Wings didn't have the best of
regular-seasons in 1965-66, finishing just four games
over 500, but we upset Chicago in the first round of the
playoffs, and suddenly the newspapers were filled with
stories about how I had a good chance of winning my
first Stanley Cup. When I watched all the attention
Ray Bourque got when the Colorado Avalanche and
New Jersey Devils reached the Stanley Cup Final in
2001, it certainly brought back memories of 1966.
Hockey didn't come close to getting the national
attention that it does today, but my quest for the
Stanley Cup in my 20th season was certainly a storyline
in the series. At that time, only Dit Clapper, Gordie
and myself had played 20 NHL seasons, and Clapper
and Gordie had won championships. The build-up
intensified when we won the first two games in
Montreal to claim a 2-0 lead in the best-of-seven series.
In Game 1, I had scored a second-period goal to give us
a 2-1 lead and young Henderson, who six years later
would be a national Canadian hero by netting the
series-winning goal at the Summit Series, scored the
eventual game winner in the 3-2 win. In Game 2, we
beat Montreal 5-2 and Crozier was really starting to
play brilliantly. With the series returning to Detroit, we
thought we were in great shape, but in Game 3

Canadiens beat us 4-2 after we had taken a 1-0 lead in that game. We would have still been fine if we won Game 4, but Ralph Backstrom's third period goal gave them a 2-1 win and tied the series. They hammered us 5-1 in Game 5, but we really felt we could force a Game 7 in Montreal. We believed we would win Game 6, Floyd Smith had scored midway through the third period to send that contest into overtime. That led to one of the most frustrating moments of my career. In overtime, Henri Richard was credited with scoring the series winning goal on what can charitably be called a controversial goal.

Most of the players knew he had gloved the puck into the net with his hand. Crozier had the best view of it all, and he said as much after the game. Crozier's anger was directed more at referee Frank Udvari than it was at Richard. Crozier believed Udvari wasn't in position to make the call.

Funny how often Udvari ended up being a thorn in my side at various points in my career. Udvari and I always seemed to have a running feud. We had been yapping at each other for years. He was the referee I shoved years before in an incident that I certainly regretted. In 1963, he gave me a ten-minute misconduct (and a $25 fine that was big in those days) during a playoff game. I was completely stunned because I wasn't even complaining when he slapped me with the call. He whistled a penalty on my teammate, Marcel Pronovost, for tripping my old nemisis Stan Mikita in the third period of Game 5. My mouth just happened to be open, and Udvari looked at me and said, "Don't say a word because Voss (NHL referee-in-chief Carl Voss) told him after the first period that he should have fined me $25 for not giving me a misconduct in the first period."

At that point, all I said was, "Maybe he should have fined you that $25." Boom. He's pointing me to the box. Can you imagine getting put in the box for something that mild? I was even smiling when I said it.

One summer, I remember being at a charity golf tournament with Udvari, and I had to hold him so he could get his ball out of a creek. The following season in the first game he slapped me with a misconduct, and I yelled, "I should have let you fall in that creek." So it was only fitting that this important game in my career should have Udvari's influence present.

To give you an idea of how close that series was, consider that Crozier won the Conn Smythe Trophy as the post-season MVP. According to newspaper accounts, Richard was a humble victor. If you read between the lines, Richard, talked sheepishly about his game-winning heroics. Sportswriter Bob Pennington's column in the Toronto newspaper said Richard implied that he had not played well in the series, and that the game-winning tally had not been deserved. Richard called it a lucky one. As painful as that game was, when it was over I knew immediately what needed to be done. What the Red Wings management, coaches or my teammates didn't know as we entered the dressing room after the game, was that I had skated over to Edna who was sitting in the stands in tears.

" Honey," I said, "you have just seen me play my last NHL game."

I kept my promise about making her the first to know when I was going to retire.

Chapter 8

The Detroit Red Wings weren't as prepared for my retirement as I was. A few days after I retired, Detroit general manager, Sid Abel, was on the phone trying to convince me to play again.

Once the season began, he was still trying to coax me out of retirement. He called me every couple of weeks just to see how I liked coaching at the junior rinks.

The Red Wings were clearly hurting on defense that season. In addition to my absence, they were trying to cope with the loss of Doug Barkley, whose career had been ended by a high stick. There are 120 minutes of playing time available for defensemen in a hockey game, and the Red Wings had lost two guys who were logging about 70 of those minutes. Gary Bergman was the teams best returning defensemen, and he was only in his second season. Detroit had slipped into last place and the Red Wings were desperate.

Sid even came to Edmonton to talk to me, and when I came back in the house smiling Edna said she was convinced I had signed another two-year contract.

I had told Sid that I didn't want to come back.

The truth was I enjoyed coaching the youngsters, and I certainly liked living full-time in Edmonton. This was certainly a more stable situation for my family.

In the fall of 1966, Brenda was 13 and Judy was 11. Donna had just turned 9 in August and our youngest, Sandy, was six. This was the first time in their lives that they would finish the school year in the same city in which they began it. They could become involved in activities year-round, instead of entering programs and friendships knowing they would be gone in another six months. Anyone who has children appreciates the level of strain that places on them.

I can't say for sure what made me quit that season, but it was just clear to me that it was time to start a new phase of my life.

At that point the Red Wings still had a very fine hockey club, and I certainly believed they had a chance to contend for the Stanley Cup. However that never entered into my thinking when I decided to retire. Neither did the money.

When I retired, my yearly salary was about $35,000, certainly an excellent wage for that era, but not in the same league with today's athletes. The job with the Edmonton Oil Kings paid $22,000 (Canadian) and that seemed like enough money. Edna's money management skill had served us well. We owned a cottage that was mortgage free, and we only owed about $6,000 on our house. Through investments and selling our golf range property, we had saved some money. We weren't rich, but we would be comfortable.

Many players from my era had nasty fights with management over money. I experienced my share of head butting over wages with general managers, but to be honest, my negotiations were small skirmishes compared to some of the tales I've heard.

In those days, no one knew what other players were making. We didn't ask. We didn't tell. Therefore you couldn't use other players as a barometer to determine what you should be earning. I couldn't march into Rangers GM office and say I heard that Tim Horton, or Doug Harvey, or John Doe is making $25,000 and I'm in their league as a player so I should be earning as much as they are. Patrick clearly would have said I was mistaken about their salaries, whether I was or not, and then he would have told me he couldn't afford to pay that kind of money.

In the Original Six era the only measuring stick a player used to determine his salary was his own level of play. If your play had improved, or you had achieved more than you had in the previous season, you thought you deserved a raise. That's how it worked in those days. That's why I was shocked when I received my 1953-54 contract offer from the Blackhawks and it spelled out that they wanted to pay me the same $11,000 they had paid me the season before, even though I had been named captain and named to the second-team NHL All-Star team. Even the bonuses were the same.

The mail carrier had brought the contract to me just as I was pulling out of my driveway to start a vacation to the Rocky Mountains with Edna and Brenda, who wasn't even five months old yet. What galled me was that team president Bill Tobin even congratulated me in a letter for making the All-Star team, but still didn't offer me a raise.

The more I drove the more perturbed I became. Edna and I decided I would write a letter to Blackhawks Tobin and ask for a $3,000 raise. I sent the letter on stationary from Jasper Park Lodge, and the postmark was from there as well.

Tobin immediately sent me back a letter.

Dear Bill:

Maybe you have gotten dizzy from walking the floor with your baby or the altitude in the mountains must have gone to your head for asking for that kind of money.

Sincerely,

Bill Tobin

I ended up missing a week of training camp, and I didn't get my $3,000 raise. Tobin did eventually give me a modest increase and agreed to give me more favorable bonus clauses.

Sometimes it wasn't just the salary that was the issue. Rangers GM Muzz Patrick and I once battled over the cost of airline tickets for my family. Every year Edna packed up the children and our belongings and began the cross-country trek from Edmonton to New York, and it occurred to me that it would be easier if she could fly first class.

"No way," Muzz said. "I can't start that. If I start doing that, then every player will want the same."

I looked him in the eye, and said, I'm not going to tell anybody, Muzz. But that's what I want. It's a chore for Edna to come out here, and that will only cost you $600 or $700.

Eventually he gave in, and true to my word I didn't tell my teammates.

My real trouble with Muzz came over the formation of the NHL Players Association. I was one of the original player representatives that met with NHL President, Clarence Campbell, and Connie Smythe at the All-Star game in Montreal in 1956-57.

Ironically, Detroit winger Ted Lindsay, who was known for stirring up trouble on the ice, proved he could create a stir off the ice. He did a great job of getting players organized to form the NHLPA. Another irony of Lindsay's willingness to become a labor organizer was that he was already managing two successful businesses in the Detroit area and clearly understood the management perspective. Everyone hated Lindsay as a player because he was a mean son of a gun. He would carve you up, and no one played more aggressively than "Terrible" Ted. But players from my era respected the job he did in rallying the players together for this cause.

Our issues were the same issues that had rallied employees in other walks of life. We wanted a guaranteed pension. We wanted some measure of security beyond our retirement date. We wanted to share in the product of our labor. Essentially, we felt as if owners were making a pile of money, and we weren't getting much of it.

When we met at the All-Star game with Clarence Campbell, my recollection is that the original representatives included Lindsay (representing Detroit), Fernie Flamen (Boston), Tod Sloan (Toronto) and Doug Harvey (Montreal). I represented the New York Rangers.

At that first meeting, Toronto Maple Leafs president, Conn Smythe, tried to bully us. "We treat you so good," he yelled. "And this is the thanks we get. If you unionize I guarantee that you won't like the consequences. You don't know how good you have it."

We understood more than Smythe realized. Although we didn't exchange salary information, we all had our own individual negotiation experiences that helped sour us on the idea that management was doing us any favors. We knew the price of tickets, and we looked at the attendance figures in the scoring summaries. You didn't need to view a spread sheet to figure out that owners weren't hurting, even though general managers were constantly whining that if they gave us an additional $1,000 per season it was going to topple the team's shaky financial structure. We didn't know exactly what other players were making, but newspaper columnists would point out occasionally that general managers had no remorse for ignoring the league's $6,500 minimum salary requirement from time to time. Borderline NHL players were particularly vulnerable to low-balling.

Smythe's verbal shelling created a certain measure of uneasiness, but it wasn't going to dissuade anyone in that room. What Smythe underestimated was our resolve, the same courage, conviction and bravado that were staples of our performance on the ice helped us come together as an association.

Unity wasn't achieved instantly. Rumors swirled that the Detroit Red Wings, Lindsay's former team, weren't 100% behind the association. And Smythe did his best to intimidate the Maple Leafs, hoping they would vote against formation. He used strong-arm tactics including telling all of the Maple Leafs that if they formed an association that they would become robots and that ultimately every player would be paid the same wage, regardless of their performance level.

It's certainly not hard to believe that Smythe went to a few players and promised to take care of them financially, if they helped quash unionism. When the first vote was taken with the Maple Leafs, the media reported that the count was 10-7 in favor of the association. (The presumption is that Smythe leaked the voting results to the media). The closeness of the vote only encouraged Smythe's union-busting attitude.

But Sloan, who had been with the Maple Leafs for seven years at that point, mounted his own campaign to unify the Maple Leafs under the NHLPA flag. He defied Smythe's rhetoric with his own well-chosen words. The next time the Maple Leafs voted it was 18-0.

Those of us who participated in the start-up of the association paid a price beyond our original $100 dues. Some paid for others. The summer after Lindsay began lobbying for the formation of the association, he was traded from the first place Red Wings to the last place Blackhawks. Glenn Hall, who had been at odds with general manager Jack Adams, went with Lindsay in the deal that brought Johnny Wilson, Hank Bassen, Forbes Kennedy and Bill Preston to the Red Wings. If you have any doubt that deal was made to punish Lindsay and Hall, consider that Lindsay was second in the NHL in scoring the season before. Hall had a 2.21 goals-against in 1956-57.

New York Rangers' general manager, Muzz Patrick, also became grumpier because of the formation of NHLPA, and he wasn't shy about ridiculing the organization. He wasn't happy that I agreed to be the player representative.

Late one night as the Rangers were on a train to Montreal, Muzz was feeling his liquor and started hollering as he was making his way through the cars.

"Where is that son of a gun who is trying to start

this union," he was yelling? "Bill Gadsby, where are you?" Goaltender Gump Worsley, forward Andy Hebenton and I were together and I yelled to the guys, "Hurry, jump in bed and pretend like you are asleep."

When Patrick enters our berth, he began to bellow, "You aren't asleep Gadsby, and I want a few answers about this players association."

Feigning as if I'm half asleep rubbing my eyes I say to Patrick, "Geez, Muzz, we've got a big game tomorrow. We can talk about this after the game."

Meanwhile, Gump Worsley is giggling and I look down and my covers are pulled up and my pants and shoes are showing.

"All right," Patrick said. "But I want this ironed out tomorrow."

Of course he never brought it up the following day. Did it change my relationship with the Rangers' management? Probably, but I don't think it had an impact on the decision to trade me to the Detroit Red Wings a few years later.

The Red Wings always seemed to treat me fairly, including owner Bruce Norris who genuinely seemed to enjoy talking to me.

Jack Adams was a curmudgeon who watched the team's finances as if anything left over would be going into his pocket, but here's a story about Adams that may shock many who had to deal with him for a contract.

At a team get-together before the 1961-62 season, Jack Adams said he was giving me a $2,500 raise.

"I still don't think you are making enough," Adams said to me. "If you have a good year, man to man, I'm telling you that I will give you another

$2,500." But that's strictly between us.

At the end of the season there was always a going away party, and that's when Adams would show up with stacks of envelopes that contained the bonus money for the season. When he saw me he said, "You had a helluva year," and he gave me an envelope that had that $2,500 he had promised me.

The Red Wings fairness to me is why I was willing to listen when Norris called me at Christmas time, 1966-67, with the hope of convincing me to come back and play.

"Hey, moneybags," Norris said as I came on the line. "We need you. We need you to come back."

My resistance was firm. "I'm not in shape," I argued. "And I really like what I'm doing here coaching. I'm having a good time."

Bruce played his trump card. "I''ll give you just what you made last season just to play a half-season," he said. " Think it over and I will get Sid to call you."

That was a tempting offer, but my resolve was firm. This wasn't about the money. It was about staying in Edmonton. It was doing something I liked, coaching, and I could continue doing that for another 20 or 25 years.

Bruce Norris realized that he wasn't getting anywhere, and we said goodbye on good terms. To be honest, I certainly didn't think I would have any more dealings with the Detroit Red Wings. I was reasonably sure I was going to spend the rest of my working days and beyond in Canada in general; in Edmonton specifically.

Life has a tendency to throw you a curve, as I found out at the end of the 1967-68 season when Norris called me again. This time he wasn't asking me to put on my skates. He was asking me to move to Detroit and coach in 1968-69.

As much as we liked it in Edmonton, the coaching offer was one that got me excited. I would be back in the NHL with yet another opportunity to win a Stanley, coaching several former teammates and players I trusted and enjoyed being around. If I took this job, I would be coaching the best line in hockey, the second Production Line of Frank Mahovlich, Alex Delvecchio and Gordie Howe.

I had come to believe that I could be a pretty good coach. People forget that in my last seasons with the Red Wings Gordie and I were considered playing assistant coaches. Back when Sid Abel was running the show in Detroit, I subbed for him a handful of times as head coach and never lost. In my first year as a junior coach the Oil Kings finished first. I enjoyed coaching the kids, but it wasn't the same as coaching at the NHL level. I was excited about this, and Edna knew it.

The decision to move back to Michigan was certainly one of the most difficult life choices Edna and I have faced, because our two oldest girls were now teen-agers. Brenda, as I recall, even had her first boyfriend. Donna and Sandy were still young enough that another move would seem like another adventure. We also knew that if I accepted the coaching job, it would devastate Brenda and Judy. Their lives would be disrupted again and this time the disruption would come during a period of their lives when consistency was important. They were both just starting to find their way in life and starting to develop close personal friendships. They were starting to emerge as young adults. We understood my potential employment move to Detroit constituted trauma for my oldest daughters.

Initially, Edna suggested that it might be best for me to go to Detroit, and for her to stay in Edmonton with the girls. Her parents, Lars and Bertha Anfindsen, had always been good about watching the girls, and Edna was sure they wouldn't mind watching them if she flew up to Michigan twice a month. The Anfindsens always went out of their way to accommodate our logistically nightmarish lifestyle. When we would arrive home every spring after the completion of the NHL season, we would walk into a house that was ready to be occupied. The cupboards and refrigerator would be filled with fresh food, and the home would be maintained as if we had lived there all year round.

When Edna told her mother she was thinking about staying in Edmonton with the children while I went to Michigan, Bertha Anfindsen responded with a simple story with a pointed message.

Bertha Anfindsen explained that every Sunday the Anfindsens would come over to our house in Edmonton just to check out security and make sure there were no problems. They would sit in the kitchen and drink coffee, but Bertha insisted those Sunday visits to our house brought her no special joy because we weren't there. She never marveled about what a nice house we owned as she sat sipping her coffee.

"This house really wasn't a home when you weren't here," Bertha told her daughter. "If you aren't there, it's just a house."

Edna and I had always talked about how much we enjoyed our Edmonton house, but what Mother Anfindsen was saying was that as much as we loved Edmonton what we really liked more was being there together as a family, and that family feeling would disappear if we were living in two separate homes. How special would our home in Edmonton be if I was living by myself in the Detroit area? Bertha was a very wise woman.

No one was more appreciative of her advice than me because I wasn't excited about going to Michigan without my family. Men don't often reveal their feelings but most men feel as I do, that it's difficult to do your job unless you feel comfortable with your home life. There is no doubt it was much easier for me to perform as a NHL hockey player because I knew that Edna was at home taking care of my children. A stable home life can be as crucial to a player as a booming slap shot. Certainly I witnessed players who had trouble performing on the ice because there was trouble at home. I liked coming home.

Edna knew that I didn't like the idea of leaving my family in Edmonton, and my feelings, coupled with her mothers words of wisdom, led her to the conclusion that the entire family would have to be moved.

Before accepting the job, I had to make one more call. I called Gordie Howe to make sure that he didn't have any designs on that job. Gordie was my closest friend on the team, and I respected him more than any player I've ever met. I respected the way he handled himself, on and off the ice. My kids think of him as Uncle Gordie.

Gordie told me that he still planned to play, and he was glad that I was coming. He told me all the Red Wings, many of whom I had played with, would be happy to have me behind the bench.

Colleen immediately grabbed the phone and pledged to help Edna anyway she could. By the time the conversation had ended, Colleen had given us the Howe home to use while they were in Toronto, and hooked us up with a realtor to find a house.

It's funny what you remember, because I remember that we looked at 67 homes before we found one we loved. I also remember that Brenda wouldn't even look at the home when we drove by it for the first time in the summer.

With Norris having called me late in the 1967-68 season, I was able to scout the Red Wings as they closed out the season. I didn't like what I saw while watching those games.

My concerns were spelled out when I was introduced as the Red Wings head coach in June of that season.

I watched several games the previous year and noticed there weren't too many bodies from the other team flying around, I said, "I expect to change that."

And I made it clear about the kind of players I wanted. I'd rather have a player that is 70 percent hustle and 30 percent talent than the other way. I'm going to demand an all-out effort.

Despite the Red Wings two consecutive seasons out of the playoffs and a last-place finish in 1967-68, I thought I could turn the team around right away. The season didn't go quite as well as I expected. We did go from 12 games under .500 to two games over .500 (33-31-12) but we still missed the playoffs. That was unacceptable to me, but Norris and Abel were quite pleased with how much better the Red Wings had played in 1968-69 than they had the previous season. We were relatively optimistic about the 1969-70 season, and Norris told me I had done a good job.

In my mind, we had some rough moments that season, particularly against Western Division teams. We were only in the second season of expansion, and the

Eastern Division teams were still expected to dominate against the newer clubs.

After we lost 6-3 to the Pittsburgh Penguins on Christmas night, I told the players they were all playing like Santa Clauses because they were all standing in front of their net giving out gifts to the opposing team.

The guys also convinced me to go out early to California so they could get acclimated and then we were bombed for 12 goals by the California Golden Seals and the Los Angeles Kings. I vowed there would be no more of that.

We had traded for the rights to Carl Brewer and Brian Conacher before that season, and then Brewer decided to coach in Finland and Conacher decided to retire at age 27. We could have used those two, particularly Brewer on defense. I thought we were just two players short of being a playoff team and a contender.

On the home front, the situation with my girls started out poorly. The two younger girls didn't have any problems adjusting, but the two older girls, as we had predicted, took much longer to find their place. Once they got into school, Judy started to make friends immediately and she began to adjust. Brenda worried us. She would simply come home from school, look for letters from her friends in Edmonton, and then just sleep all the time. She was lethargic, uninterested, and more than once I worried about what I had done to her.

Edna went up to Southfield High School to talk to a counselor, and this wonderful counselor took a special interest in Brenda. He got her a job in the high school office where she met a friend. That helped. Trying to be good parents, we thought sending her home to Alberta for Christmas would help. However she had such a good time there that she begged us to let her stay there for the rest of the school year.

We finally convinced her to come home, with the understanding that if she still wanted to return to Edmonton she could go to college there. (She eventually made friends in Michigan, and decided not to attend college there.)

That seemed to calm our life down quite a bit. My family was adjusting. The team was adjusting. I felt they were improving. Owner Bruce Norris seemed happy with my work. When I came to Detroit, we didn't even get a contract because that's the way Norris liked to operate. That didn't bother me because Norris had always taken care of me. He had always been fair to me, and I couldn't foresee that changing. When I looked back, the NHL coaching job was perfect for me. I enjoyed my job. I thought I did it well. My best friend was the star of the team. The situation seemed almost too good to be true. And it was because Norris wasn't the man I thought he was.

Chapter 9

In hockey, the most dangerous hits are those that a player doesn't see coming. After 20 seasons of constantly keeping my head up as a National Hockey League defenseman, it is ironic that the most injurious blow I ever received occurred after I quit playing.

The blindside smack came October 16, 1970, and it wasn't delivered by a man wearing a NHL sweater. He was wearing a $500 suit and sipping a cocktail.

Looking back at the start of the 1969-70 campaign, I remember having as much optimism about my Detroit Red Wings squad than a coach had a right to have. My No. 1 line of Frank Mahovlich, Alex Delvecchio and Gordie Howe had combined for 118 goals the season before. Carl Brewer had come out of retirement to play for us, and he was really going to help our defense.

Peter Stemkowski, whose injury had hurt us badly in the stretch run in 1968-69, was healthy and I had a good feeling that 22-year-old center Garry Unger was on the verge of a breakthrough season.

Despite the fact that the Boston Bruins had this

free-wheeling Bobby Orr kid and an exceptional team
and the Blackhawks were good, I thought we could win
the Stanley Cup. Needless to say I wasn't surprised
when we were 8-1 during the preseason and opened the
regular season with wins over Toronto Maple Leafs and
the Chicago Blackhawks. At that point in my life,
things couldn't have been any better.

It would have been perfect if Detroit owner
Bruce Norris hadn't decided to fire me right then.

Considering the teams 2-0 record, it's safe to
presume I never saw this bullet coming. After we had
beaten the Blackhawks, Norris was gushing about how
strong the team looked. He loved beating the
Blackhawks, especially in Chicago Stadium, because his
brother Jim owned that team. That night he put his
arm around me and said, " Bill, you really got these
guys going."

"Bruce," I replied, "We are going to have a great
year."

About 48 hours later I was unemployed;
probably the only NHL coach ever to be dismissed when
his team had a 1.000 winning percentage.

Not surprising, Norris had a martini idling in
front of him when I entered his office not one hour
before we were supposed to take the ice against the
Minnesota North Stars. It hadn't alarmed me to be
summoned because Norris always wanted to talk about
players. He would pour alcohol down his gullet and
words would come back out in the form of orders about
particular players. I figured he wanted to complain
about Gary Bergman again, or to gush about some
rookie in our system. It never occurred to me that he
was about to give me a pink slip. The whole
conversation lasted about 60 seconds. "I am making a

change," he said. " I'm putting Sid (Abel) behind the bench." " We are 2-0 and we have a terrific hockey club," I said. "Why would you fire me?"

"I run a lot of corporations," he mumbled, "and sometimes I just have a feeling of when I need to make a change."

"So that's it?," I asked. "I'm done?"

" That's it," he said. "Thanks for your time."

It was the most shocking moment of my life. I left without saying another word. Had I not been stunned I would have had more to say to him. But that would come later.

When I walked out of his office I had to walk through the Olympia room, where I coincidentally ran into Edna. She could see something was wrong immediately and when I gave her the news you could see her legs quiver. I could just see it in her eyes. All the years of being a good soldier had meant nothing. We had packed, re-packed, moved the kids in and out of schools all the years I played, and now when we finally thought we had some stability in our lives, it was washed away callously by a man with his fingers around one of his frequent cocktails.

The news of my firing couldn't have been spread more quickly if Norris had announced it over the public address system. It roared around Olympia like a bush fire.

Edna immediately headed to the washroom where the tears could flow more privately. Coincidently, Edna had ridden down to Olympia early with Gordie and Colleen so that Colleen could show her Gordie's new office. He was starting a business as an insurance representative. Colleen had run into some of Norris' cronies, and Edna had excused herself to go see some old friends who were celebrating a wedding anniversary that night. When Edna had left, Norris' friends told Colleen that I was in Norris' office getting fired. Colleen was steamed. She went looking for Edna, and found her in the bathroom and did what she could to console her.

Edna was far more concerned about our two daughters who were at that game, and Edna immediately went to find them, not wanting them to hear the news from strangers. It was too late. They already knew, and they were quite upset.

After talking with Edna for just a few moments, I ran into my old Chicago Blackhawks teammate, John Mariucci, who was then working for the North Stars. He had gotten the news in the North Stars dressing room and had come to pass along his condolences.

About the only people in the building who didn't seem to know, were the Detroit players. With shock now giving way to anger, I headed toward the Red Wings dressing room to talk to Abel and assistant GM Baz Bastien about the situation. I had to know why I was fired. I just wanted a reason, or even some rationale for the firing.

The team was on the ice for warm-ups when I entered the room, but Big Frank Mahovlich was still in there.

"Bill," he said. "I've got a Charlie Horse, and I'm going to try to go tonight, but I don't know if I can."

"Don't talk to me," I said. "I just got fired."

Mahovlich's jaw dropped to his knees. " What is going on around here?" he asked.

As he limped down the hallway, he screamed, "Whoever is in charge around here, I would like to tell them that I don't know if I can play tonight."

Abel and Bastien were in the medical room, and before I could say a word Sid blurted out, " I had nothing to do with this. This was Bruce's decision."

Although I didn't stay around to watch the game that night, the newspaper reports of the game the next day were that when the Red Wings fell behind 3-1 in the second period, they looked disorganized with Abel behind the bench. The crowd began to chant, "We want Gadsby." " We want Gadsby."

The North Stars eventually won the game 3-2. Red Wings' defenseman, Ron Harris, was quoted as saying, " the players were shook up by the firing because we had a good bond between us."

One of my strengths as a coach was that I tried to be honest with players. No malarkey. And that wasn't easy with Norris in charge. Generally when players weren't performing as well as I liked, I didn't have any problem telling them.

God bless Gordie Howe who really stood up for me. "It just makes me sick," he told reporters about the firing. "There was no inkling this was coming. They just fired him. No warning. I wonder if I still have a job on this team. It just makes you wonder."

As surprised as I was by my dismissal, I can't say that I never believed Bruce Norris was incapable of impulsive behavior. I had experienced some of that during my first season behind the bench, particularly when it came to personnel moves. Everyone believes that New York Yankees boss, George Steinbrenner, was the original meddlesome team owner. But I can tell you that long before Steinbrenner was calling Billy Martin in the dugout and telling him what he thought about Martins managerial decisions, Norris was calling me

during the games and trying to tell me whom he wanted
to see on the ice.

Early in my first season, the phone started
ringing. There was a phone at the end of the bench and
a light would turn red when Norris wanted to speak to
me. Trainer Lefty Wilson would see it first and then let
me know. As soon as I would pick up the phone, I could
hear the alcohol talking.

"Bill," Norris would say. "Why do you have
Gary Bergman playing so much?"

"For heavens sake," I replied, "Bergie is playing
well. He's the best I have. Who else do I have to put
in?"

"I don't care," Norris would say. "I don't want
to see Bergman out there." Then he would hang up.

It didn't matter to Norris that I told him
Bergman was playing well. For some reason he just
didn't like the late Bergman. This is the same Bergman
who two years later was chosen as one of the leagues
best defenseman to play for the NHL All-Stars against
the All-Stars in the famed 1972 Summit Series.

The night the calls started coming I sought out
Abel between periods and told him Norris had called me
four times in the first two periods. He wasn't surprised
by the calls, or that Norris had singled out a single
player. Abel told me that was Norris' usual procedure.

Norris and his entourage (that's what I always
called them) would sit in his small suite to watch the
game and if the team wasn't winning or if the Red
Wings weren't sharp, one of his cronies would begin
badmouthing a player. Perhaps to impress his buddies,
Norris would immediately be on the phone and demand
that the player be punished.

The way Sid described the scene to me it was like

some college fraternity party with free flowing booze and the guests egging Norris on. Maybe it was fun and games to them, but it wasn't to me. These athletes were my players, and the vast majority of them worked their tails off to get where they were.

Abel agreed with me that Bergman had been playing fine, but he also told me you gotta do what Bruce says to a certain extent.

Even though I thought Bergie was playing fine, I did sit him out that night, and I sat him a couple of other nights, because this was Norris' team and I'd always felt loyalty should be part of this business. I did wonder, however, whether Norris had any understanding of the game. I became more convinced of that the night Norris approached me between the first and second period, during a game in Pittsburgh, and demanded that Dean Prentice not play any more that night.

"Why?" I asked. "Are you trading him? He's one of our hottest players. He's got six goals in nine games and he and Bruce McGregor are our best penalty killers."

Norris said he wasn't trading Prentice, but he didn't want to see Prentice out there any more. End of message.

When the second period started, I took Prentice off his regular line. I put Gordie out there to kill penalties with McGregor. I could feel him looking at me all the time, wondering whether I had lost my mind. We had played seven seasons together with the New York Rangers, and had always come ready to play every single night. He did the job the way it was supposed to be done. In the third period, I ran into some penalty problems, and I used him a couple of shifts. But I knew he wasn't going to let this pass.

When we got on the team bus to head to the airport, he plopped down on the seat next to me.

"What was going on tonight?" he asked simply.

"I just didn't think you had the jump tonight," I lied through my teeth.

"What do I have to do for you?" he asked.

I had no answer. At the time, I didn't believe it was proper to disclose the owners thoughts about the player. I thought that was just between Norris and I. That conversation with Prentice just tore me up, actually haunted me for years because of the respect I had for Dean as a player and as a man. Through the years I've said consistently that Prentice should have been in the Hall of Fame. Everyone in hockey understood how valuable he was.

After I was fired, I tried to phone Prentice to explain what had happened that night. But I never found him. It was years later at a celebrity golf tournament that we saw each other, and I pulled him aside and explained the truth of why I had benched him. He had just assumed that he could have been on the verge of being traded, and we didn't want to see him get hurt. I told him that wasn't the reason, and apologized for lying to him.

My patience for Norris' meddling began to wear thin as the 1968-69 season progressed. I didn't give in to him one night in Boston over the playing time of 21-year-old rookie Rene Leclerc. Maybe that was the first strike against me. Leclerc was a French Canadian kid who could fly on skates and he could stick-handle in the backseat of a Volkswagon Beetle. He had dipsy doodled his way to 31 goals and 42 assists in 55 games the previous season while playing junior hockey for the

Hamilton Red Wings. The problem was that he weighed about 138 pounds. It listed him at 160 pounds, but I swear if you had let him stay in his uniform and stood him under the shower to get him soaking wet and let him hold a dumbbell in each hand he still wouldn't weigh more than 140. He was just a wisp of a man at that point in his career.

Norris liked Leclerc for some reason and when I wasn't playing him much in this game in Boston, Norris came down and demanded to know why.

I explained to him rather calmly that the Bruins had a big physical hockey team, with players like Wayne Cashman, Ken Hodge, Ted Green, Johnny McKenzie, Derek Sanderson, not to mention Phil Esposito and Bobby Orr. If I put Leclerc out there in this game, they may kill him. Besides that we're leading 2-1 and I don't want to take a chance with a young kid out there.

Norris didn't press the issue, but you have to wonder if he filed away my insubordination for future reference. If I didn't anger him that night, I probably did later in the season when I yanked the phone out of the wall on the bench after he called me four times in one game. Lefty Wilson looked up at me and then down at the badly injured phone like I had just knocked a hornets nest down in front of me. "Bill," he said. "You should not have done that."

Nothing really came of that incident, and even though we missed the playoffs that season there wasn't any indication that my job was in jeopardy.

The only Norris move in the off-season was to hire noted Oshawa Green Gaels lacrosse coach, Jim Bishop, to do a job and wasn't really explained in great detail. Bishop had also handled the Detroit Olympics during the ill-fated National Lacrosse Association experiment in 1968. Norris apparently liked Bishop's style. If you are wondering why Norris picked a lacrosse coach to work for a hockey team, you can appreciate why the move didn't sit well with the Red Wings management, particularly general manager Sid Abel. Officially, 40-year-old Bishop's title was executive director of Olympia Stadium and the Detroit Red Wings. All Norris said to Sid, Baz and me was that Jim was going to coordinate everything in general.

To be candid, Bishop's role didn't seem all that important to me when training camp started at McMorrin Arena in Port Huron, Michigan. It didn't seem very logical that a lacrosse guru was going to be telling me much about how to coach a hockey club.

When training camp began, Bishop didn't even sit with Sid and Baz. He sat in the stands by himself and watched. We were all amused that he was always furiously scribbling notes on his pad. He spent more time writing then watching. The more we practiced, the more he wrote. I had no idea what he was writing, nor did I care until Sid came up to me after the fourth or fifth day and said Bishop had suggested to him that he didn't think players were working hard enough and he didn't think I was tough enough on them. At least the mystery was solved about what Bishop was writing about.

A couple days later, Bishop ran into me as I was leaving the dressing room and he obviously decided he had better deliver his message again in person.

"I don't think Gordie Howe and Alex Delvecchio and some of the guys are pushing themselves very hard," Bishop said. "And I think you need to be tougher on them."

Think about that. With no previous hockey background, his first recommendation to me was to be tougher on two Hall of Fame players who had combined for 186 points the previous season.

" If Gordie Howe and Alex Delvecchio are my biggest problems, I'm in really great shape," I said before walking away.

My exchange with Bishop was a sparkler compared to the major fireworks going on between Abel and Bishop. By 1969, Abel had been in professional hockey for 31 years. He had played his first season for the Red Wings in 1938-39 and had won his first Stanley Cup as a player in 1942-43. Abel had been the Red Wings general manager since 1962, and he had coached the team from 1958-59 until I was given the job in 1968-69. He wasn't about to allow a non-hockey guy to tell him how to govern hockey players. I heard arguments between Abel and Bishop in the hallway, and I wasn't surprised when Abel told me that Bishop had scheduled a management meeting. He also wanted me there, plus Doug Barkley who was Detroit's minor league coach in Fort Worth.

When we all gathered in the Port Huron Flags meeting room, before Bishop could say a word, Abel pounded his fist on the table and pointed his finger at Bishop and said that he had no authority to demand his presence at a meeting. If there were to be any more meetings Abel said he would call them. He said the meeting was over. We all got up to leave, but before we got to the door, Bishop and Abel were screaming at each other. They were nose to nose in seconds. Barkley and I had to separate them. All of this happened before we even knew why Bishop called the meeting.

Later, when training camp was over and we were

into the exhibition season, we were playing a game in Halifax, Nova Scotia. We knew Norris was coming in for the game, so Sid and I decided we would have a midnight curfew. After the game, I went out for dinner with Sid and when we came back, three players were coming into the hotel 15 minutes late for curfew. I made a mental note to deal with that in the morning. Then just my luck Norris' limousine shows up. I don't know if Norris saw them, but Bishop did and as soon as I arrived at my room the phone was ringing. It was Bishop demanding that I punish the offending players severely. I told him I would be dealing with it in my own way. I was quite firm about that.

The next day at breakfast he brought it up again, and this time I told him more forcefully that I would handle discipline matters privately with my players. Maybe he thought he had authority over me, but I didn't see it that way.

Did Bishop play a role in my ouster? The truth is, I still don't know, but I'm sure he didn't help. We were obviously resistant to his idea of meeting-oriented philosophy. He talked frequently about NFL coaches Vince Lombardi and Paul Brown, and their philosophies about coaching. After I was fired I joked to the press, "he talked about Lombardi so much that I thought Lombardi was going to be the new coach of the Detroit Red Wings."

The day after I was fired I was in the Red Wings offices to see the comptroller about financial concerns, and Bishop asked to see me. He told me to my face that he had nothing to do with Norris' decision.

Anger consumed me at that point, and I told him, "if I find out that you had anything to do with this I will be back here and spin you around this room like a cat. You will hit every wall."

To this day, my firing still has an element of mystery associated with it. Did Abel just want to return to coaching? According to Norris' quotes in the newspaper the next day, he had discussed the change with Abel for a few days, however, Abel told me this had just been Norris' decision. Did Norris have a new breed coach in mind that turned them down? Did he not like me because I yanked out the phone? Those theories have all been suggested to me, but no one knows for sure. Norris didn't share with me, or anyone, as far as I know, why he fired me.

At the press conference discussing my departure, Norris implied that I didn't communicate well enough with some of the top players, which is strange since most of those top players seemed genuinely miffed that I was fired. He kept making references to hockey becoming more sophisticated and that I wasn't the guy for the job. He said the game plan had gone astray. Whatever that means. Even reporters noted in their stories that Norris seemed vague about his rationale for my dismissal.

When we returned home that night, Edna and I sat at the kitchen table and admitted to ourselves that we had no idea what to do. We had uprooted our family just 15 months before, causing great pain for our children, particularly our oldest daughter, Brenda, who was already in high school. We did that because Bruce Norris had always been good to us. Now the man we had trusted had betrayed us.

On the night I was fired, Brenda was babysitting for the children of Gerry Abel who was Sids son. She heard the news of my firing on the television, and she was hysterical by the time we returned home.

I had no idea that night what I wanted to do with my life, but probably by the time I walked out of Norris' office, October 16, 1969, I knew in my heart I would never coach again.

Questions swirled about as Edna discussed our future in stark terms. Should we go back to Edmonton? Should I try to get another NHL scouting job? Should I quit hockey all together?

Shortly after the game was over, at about 11 p.m. there was a knock on the door, and Gordie and Colleen had arrived with beer and pizza to commiserate with us. John Curran, another friend who owned a crane rental company, and his wife, Jackie were also there.

We all sat at that table until 5 a.m. trying to analyze what had happened. Gordie and Colleen were the friends they had always been. At some point that night, Curran told me to come and see him to discuss a job with his company as a sales representative and shortly thereafter I decided to take the job. It's a move I never regretted.

My assumption was that I would never see Norris again, but fate obviously has a sense of humor or a cruel side, depending upon your perspective.

Curran was a wonderful, generous man who owned a beautiful vacation home in the high-priced community of Ocean Reef, near Key Largo, Florida. He invited Edna and I to come down for a visit later that same winter. One night, we had a few drinks and went to have supper at the Ocean Reef Lodge. The night air was warm and peaceful. My wife and good friends were with me and my life couldn't be much better. We had a few more drinks and I couldn't have been farther removed from my days as a NHL hockey coach.

Bruce Norris was the last person in the world that I would have thought about at that moment. Imagine my astonishment when he walked into the Ocean Reef Lodge. Better yet, imagine his astonishment. When the manager started walking Norris and his entourage down to a table near ours and he spotted me, he looked like he was going to collapse.

Always able to read my mind, Edna grabbed my leg and said, " Bill, don't do anything here."

I said I wouldn't, but we both knew that I might not mean it.

Probably, Norris was thinking, How could Bill Gadsby be hobnobbing in my stomping grounds? Before Norris could take another step, I was in front of him, confronting him straight-forward, no different than I had any opponent I had ever faced in my 20 years as a NHL player. I could see in Norris' eyes that at that moment he would have preferred to be anywhere but right in front of me. It was the same look of dread that opponents used to get when they realized they had ticked off Black Jack Stewart in Chicago or Gordie Howe in Detroit.

"I need to see you for a minute, Bruce," I said.

"Oh, no, Bill, right now isn't good because I have people here."

My voice was probably too loud, and people were watching, but I didn't care.

"If you are any kind of a man, you will give me three or four minutes of your time," I said. "I want to know why you fired me."

Obviously embarrassed, Norris quickly made apologies to his guests, and motioned toward a hallway. Once out of the main dining area, I repeated my question, "Why did you fire me? I was 2-0, 8-1 in training camp. How could we have been better than that? You told me the game before that I was doing a terrific job. This doesn't add up."

He started talking about all his corporations, and about how he always knew when it was time to make a change. I quickly cut him off, and asked again, "Why did you fire me?"

"This isn't the place for this," Norris said. "I'm down here for a while. Let's have lunch tomorrow. You can come down to the water and we can have lunch on the Pretty Red Wings"

The invitation to meet him on his boat escalated my anger.

"I don't care about you or your boat," I said. "We aren't having lunch on your boat. I never want to see you again. Let's do it right here."

That's exactly what I said. My anger was boiling over, and when he started giving some verbal tap dance around the question, I grabbed him around the throat. Just then I realized that J.J. and Edna were watching down the hall, and Edna said sharply, " Bill, don't you do anything."

At that point, I just pushed his head against the wall and said, "You're not a man."

That was the last time I ever talked to Norris. He owned the Red Wings until he sold them to Mike and Marian Ilitch in 1980. In the 1970s under Norris' stewardship, the team missed the playoffs nine out of 10 seasons. He died January 1, 1986, and to my knowledge he never really explained to anyone in great detail about why he fired me.

Whatever the reason, Norris' decision changed my life. A couple of weeks after I was fired, St. Louis Blues owner Harry Ornest called me and offered me a job. We had played baseball against each other in Edmonton years before, and we had mutual respect for one other. He wanted me to come and work for him as a scout or a coach, and we would see what would develop from there.

Minnesota owner Walter Bush also called me about the possibility of coaching the North Stars. The door was open for me to resume my career, but I really wasn't enthused about re-entering that world. Edna sensed my reluctance about continuing in this profession. She has always had an intuition about what's the right move and wrong move. She lays the cards on the table.

Edna asked all the right questions. Did I want to move again? Would it be fair to move the children again? Did I want to put my fate in the hands of another owner? And what about job security? J.J. Curran was offering me a great job with a guaranteed future. What guarantees did I have in the hockey world?

She is an astute woman, and she knew the answers before the questions were out of her mouth. She knew that the firing had been so devastating that it had probably soured me on coaching for good. We had sold our business in Edmonton and gave up a terrific junior coaching job for a handshake deal with Bruce Norris. As it turned out a handshake wasn't as sacred to Norris as it was to me.

That firing certainly has haunted me for years. The only solace I ever had was that unlike in most sports coach firing situations, where the general sentiment is good riddance, I was portrayed by the media as being a victim. In support of me, fans brought banners and signs to the games for the next few weeks.

They actually staged a protest at the game, picketing Olympia on my behalf. Can you imagine that?

Norris certainly hadn't been prepared for the public backlash that followed my dismissal. In the weeks after I was let go, I was sent a letter from the Red Wings saying I would be paid for the remainder of the season. Norris had added in pencil that payments would stop if I made any derogatory comments about the organization.

In the summer of 2001, I ran into Brewer at a golf outing and he said he had always regretted not taking a stand on my behalf.

"If I had my thoughts together," he told me not long before he died, " I wouldn't have taken the ice that night."

Always a rebel, Brewer really might have done just that if he thought about it. It probably wouldn't have done much good, but the sentiment was appreciated.

When the firing occurred I was 43. Given all the personal hardships I had endured by that point in my life, including the Athenia sinking, the polio and my business partner Clarence Mohers death from a heart attack, there was reason to hope that I would not ever face any personal crisis as difficult as the ones I had already faced. That hope turned out not to be well founded.

Chapter 10

On October 16, 1988, the ringing of a doorbell altered my life more than any event except my marriage to Edna.

When the door swung open, my four daughters were standing there, along with three of my sons-in-law. As close as I am to my children, this was an alarming sight.

This was no holiday. No grandchildren were with them. None of them were smiling.

"We need to have a chat with you Dad," said Brenda's husband, Dennis Golembiewski.

As we all sat around the kitchen table, the same kitchen table where we spent many joyous family gatherings, my children and their spouses gave me the best gift they had ever given me. They gave me back my dignity, and ultimately my life.

Dennis had been designated as their spokesman, and he, looked me in the eye and said, "We think you are drinking too much, and we want to take you to get some help."

Milt Schmidt's crushing check 40 years before

hadn't rocked me as severely as Dennis' words.

Having lived in the ugly world of denial for far too many years, my instincts forced me into a defensive posture.

" Sometimes I take too many drinks, but I'm not in trouble," I said. "This isn't a situation I can't handle."

Everyone in my home that night, including me, knew better.

One by one, my daughters told me their stories and observations about my drinking. My daughter, Judy, told a particularly tough story, mentioning that she had come to see me and caught me taking a nip out of a bottle of vodka that I kept stashed near my lawnmower in the garage. I knew she had witnessed my drinking that day because she had left me a note by the bottle. That note had said, "Dad, you just broke my heart."

That note had tugged at my emotions that day because I love my family very deeply, and I remember thinking, " Bill, how dumb can you be?"

Here I was sneaking out to the garage, trying to hide my drinking from Edna and my family. The silly part of that was that I wasn't really hiding it from them, because they already knew.

Edna had been keeping a diary of my drinking habits since 1979, and she had been urging me to seek help for a decade. My family also knew because my personality was changing. Alcoholism is a progressive disease, and it was starting to defeat me.

When I was sneaking around stashing bottles, the real person I was trying to hide my drinking from was myself. By pretending that no one knew I was drinking, it helped me fuel my denial of the problem.

This disease had a grip on me, and it just wouldn't let go. Even in my stronger moments when I would tell myself that I had to stop, I seemed powerless to do anything about it. I would tell myself that I could go a day without drinking, but at 8 a.m., 9 a.m., 11 a.m., or noon, I would go back to the bottle, always finding rationalization for my behavior. I would tell myself I would go two hours without drinking, but in 15 minutes the booze would be in my mouth.

When my children began this organized intervention into my drinking problem, it was easy to start trying to lie to them because I had been lying to Edna and myself for years about how much I was drinking. Alcoholics lie so often that it eventually becomes routine, like tying their shoes or combing their hair.

" How much did you have to drink?" Edna would ask me. "Just a couple," I would say. But really it would have been six, seven, or eight. The number didn't matter. What mattered was that I felt as if I needed my bottle of vodka to get through the day.

That thought was in my mind when Dennis was telling me they had talked to Detroit Red Wings physician Dr. John Finley, my long-time personal physician and family friend, and he had arranged for me to enter an alcohol rehabilitation program at Ford Hospital.

"You have two choices," Dennis said. "You can either go in voluntarily or we are going to put you there, but we would rather you go voluntarily."

The family had done their homework on alcoholism. They had been to the bookstore. They had done their research. They had talked to others who had encountered these same types of problems and had dealt with them. They had talked to experts.

Dennis had been particularly aggressive in obtaining information, and he told everyone that if I was going to be angry about this intervention, he wanted to make sure that my anger would be directed at him. He didn't want my anger to be directed toward my daughters. Dennis had compassion, even in the face of this difficult time. What I didn't know until later was that Dennis told my daughters if I wouldn't go voluntarily he was prepared to use physical force to make me go to rehabilitation. It didn't matter to Dennis that I was a Hall of Fame hockey player. It didn't matter that I once had knocked NHL tough guy Howie Young off a porch. It didn't matter to Dennis that I once had hit Tim Horton with enough force that hospitalization was required. All that mattered to him was that I was his father-in-law, and I needed to be in rehabilitation and if he had to attempt to manhandle me in order to get me into that program, he was prepared to do that.

I feel as if I'm close to all of my sons-in-law. Each of them is special to me. However, Dennis and I had hit it off because we had very similar interests. We liked many of the same hobbies. We had always talked about going deep-sea fishing. Maybe he thought we had similar ideas of looking at life. Maybe that's why he felt he had to be spokesperson. Maybe he thought I would relate to him.

This was an uncomfortable situation for all of us, and I really didn't say much. At that point, I started to talk about maybe looking at going to a program in a few days. " No," Dennis said, "we will take you tonight."

At that point, I rose from my chair and walked

away, putting my hands over my face and it instantly became clear that I needed help and more importantly that I wanted help. As I have said only to Edna, some voice in the back of my head told me, " It's time, Bill, it's time to go."

In hindsight, it's clear how I arrived at the point I needed my family to help me find my way back home. At the time, nothing was clear to me because my drinking dulled my senses. At various times, I would tell myself I didn't like what the drinking was doing to me, but I seemed powerless to do anything about it.

Each time I pledged to Edna that I was going to stop, cold turkey, or at least cut back, it actually seemed to become worse. She had been going to Alanon meetings for nine years before that intervention, and she remembers vividly coming away from those meetings thinking maybe I wasn't an alcoholic because my story didn't have the nightmarish quality of many others she heard. When she first started to go to Alanon I had a job. I went to work every day and I certainly wasn't physically abusive to anyone in my life.

Certainly the signs were there and drinking was beginning to overwhelm my life.

During my playing days, my drinking simply wasn't an issue. Certainly, I would go out with the guys, occasionally for a beer or two, but anyone who knew me back then would swear I was essentially a family man. Yes, a few nights Edna wasn't happy about how much alcohol was consumed, but in looking back, Edna says she didn't consider me an excessive drinker. In fact, she recalls quite vividly when the kids were young, we would often go right home after a game.

The difficulty really began for me after I lost my job as coach of the Red Wings and began working for John Curran. It was my job to serve as a public relations and sales representative for Curran Crane. According to my job description, I was supposed to check on the job sites to make sure everything was going okay and to entertain our customers. Part of my job was to golf with them, and to take them to Detroit Red Wings games, for example. The irony of my development into an alcoholic in that position was that one of Curran's edicts was there was to be no drinking on the job. He was adamant about that rule.

The rule was followed in the beginning, but over the course of time my attitude changed. When customers would say, "Go-ahead Bill have one." I would. Then I would have two. Before long, my drinking patterns changed to accommodate my desire for alcohol. Instead of drinking beer, I started craving hard stuff.

John Curran quickly figured out that I was violating his policy about imbibing on the job, and he confronted me. Of course I lied to him about how much I was drinking. I was in denial then, and my environment helped me become a closet drinker. Often I would be on my own with clients, and alcoholics are quite crafty about planning their days around the pursuit of drinking. I knew which clients would want to drink, and I spent more time with them. I wasn't a bar hopper, but I knew where some of my drinking friends would be, so I would stop there for one or two, and quickly it would become four or five.

On May 29, 1982, John told me he was laying me off after 12 years because business was bad. But both of us understood that my drinking was the root of my dismissal. No one had to say it. Maybe business was bad, but if I had been a sober employee, John would have tried to keep me on. That's the kind of man he was.

At that point, Edna had encouraged me to get back in the hockey school business. We had done very well in that enterprise for a number of years, however, I didn't want to do that. That was probably a sign of how unclearly I was thinking.

First, I went to work for Uni-Bond, but I didn't like it from the beginning. The salary and commissions were much lower than I had received from Curran. After five months I quit. I had it in my head that I wanted to own my own company and I saw an ad in the Detroit paper for a nuts and bolts factory called Autometrics in Allen Park. If we sunk our life savings into the plant and obtained a loan, we could swing the purchase. On October 18, 1983, we bought the business. This was a major step for us because we always paid cash for whatever we bought.

Edna says now that she went along with the idea because she thought this new venture might give me the inspiration I needed to quit drinking. While at Curran Crane, I had become bored with my job and was looking for a challenge. What we liked about the situation was that many of the company's main customers were also Curran's clients. I would be calling on people I knew.

As excited as I was about the new business, it was quickly evident that I had made a huge mistake. The landlords of our building raised the rent from $800 to $1,200 per month and everything went downhill from there. Soon there wasn't enough business to support our four employees, and we weren't drawing a penny in salary. Was it a bad business decision or did my drinking effect my ability to make it work? Maybe it was a little of both. On September 2, 1985, we sold the business for $1 just to free ourselves from the daily debts, but we still had obligations to lawyers, accountants, etc. We lost more than $100,000, essentially our life's savings, in 23 months of operation.

Those were difficult months in our house, and the drinking made the situation worse. Edna says I was never abusive as a drinker, but I was becoming increasingly more argumentative.

Again it seemed as the guardian angel was looking after me because John Curran had heard that my company was in trouble and offered me a chance to come back to work for him on December 16, 1985. It came just before Christmas, and it seemed as if everything would be fine.

It wasn't fine because I was an alcoholic and it didn't take me long to fall into old patterns. John Curran put up with my drinking for another couple of years, but both of us knew my employment was hanging by a thread.

On March 24, 1988, I was fired for the second time by Curran Crane. I came into the office and John's two sons said they needed to talk to me. Behind closed doors, they informed me they had to let me go and I would have to turn in the keys for the company car. They said they would have someone drive me home. They told me why they were letting me go, but they didn't need to. I knew.

When Edna came home, she was stunned to find me home with no car in the driveway. She remembers that when I told her what happened I was as sober as I've ever been.

At that point, we went back in the hockey school business and that was our livelihood. I functioned well enough in that capacity to make a living, but in looking back I was glad I had good instructors like my close friend Johnny Wilson, a former Red Wings player. At home I was starting to bottom out. I was hiding bottles and I started to be less social with my family. I was laying around more, and sleeping more during the day. That way I could drink at night while others were sleeping. It's a familiar pattern for drinkers.

I was less talkative than I used to be, and then I started to make up excuses for not going to family gatherings. What I know now is that I wanted to stay close to my alcohol. If Edna went to functions alone, I was free to stay home and drink.

When that started to happen, my daughters began comparing notes. That's when they decided to confront their mother about my drinking habits. They invited her to Brenda and Dennis' home two days before they confronted me.

In all the years I was drinking, Edna never threatened to leave me. The only drastic action she ever took was to tell my daughters. She knew that would rip at my heart. "Don't do that," I would tell her. "They have their own families to worry about. I will fix this myself."

Today, Edna speaks about having regrets about being my enabler. At that meeting, my daughters were angry that Edna hadn't told them what was going on, but that anger is misplaced. It was my problem, not Edna's. She was trying to help me, but I wouldn't listen.

Thankfully, we are a close family because in hindsight that intervention probably only worked because we are close. Each of my daughters believed that if they drained the alcohol from my system and forced me to confront my problem, I would once again become the daddy they knew and loved. Somewhere under the alcoholic was the same man who used to take them fishing and water skiing all day long, seven days a week at our cottage in Edmonton. Somewhere under the alcoholic was the man who would do anything to avoid hurting them. I think they knew that.

My journey to sobriety started that night, even though I actually didn't make it into rehabilitation until the following day. When we arrived at Ford Hospital, nurses drew blood and told my family I was legally drunk. The hospital staff was set to admit me when it was discovered that the hospital didn't accept my insurance. Since I had lost my job, we had been purchasing our own insurance and to save money we had switched to an HMO. Ford Hospital officials quickly determined that the only place I could be admitted was in Riverview, which was 30 miles from our home. In addition, that center couldn't admit me until the next morning.

When we got home, everyone wanted to stay with me all night. But I said it wasn't necessary, and I think they knew I meant it. Edna and I stayed up all night together. Maybe this was one of the most important nights we ever spent together. It was the first night I hadn't had a drink in a long time.

When we arrived at Riverview, it was clear this center seemed rougher around the edges than Ford Hospital. There were people from all walks of life in the center and this wasn't a white-collar alcohol rehabilitation center. Heroin addicts. Crack addicts. We were all there hoping we might break free of the monster that was enslaving us.

Edna told me later that she and our daughters

went outside, afterward, in the car and bawled because they thought they were leaving me in such a rough place.

Once inside the doors, I was told up front that I was free to walk away at any time, but if I did I couldn't come back for a lengthy period. A counselor told me I had choices to make about what kind of life I wanted, and she was willing to help me if I was willing to help myself.

I was willing to confront my demon. I didn't want to be as miserable as I had been for a decade. I wanted my life back.

To some alcoholics the talks, the movies and counseling don't take hold right away. To me the counseling was like a light showing me the way home.

While I was in rehabilitation, former Detroit Lions first-round draft pick Reggie Rogers, a promising defensive lineman, was involved in an alcohol-related accident that killed three teen-agers. He ended up serving some jail time for the accident.

I remember sitting in Riverview thinking, "that could have been me."

I never was arrested for drunk driving, nor had any alcohol-related accidents, but twice I was pulled over by police on suspicion of drunk driving. Apparently, I must have had just enough command of my senses to know I was a danger to myself and others. Each time I was pulled over it was for driving too slow, not too fast.

I can't say for sure, but my guess is that I probably had an open drink in my car when they pulled me over.

Each time the police officer recognized me or my name, they would call Edna instead of arresting me.

In both instances, Edna was told, " Your husband is having car trouble and he needs a ride home."

Edna says now that perhaps I would have been better off if the police would have arrested me because maybe I would have been in rehabilitation sooner. It's really difficult to know whether I would have been ready to accept rehabilitation at that point in my life. Some experts say it's necessary for an alcoholic to bottom out in order to begin his or her climb back. We will never know for sure.

Clearly, people in my life suspected that I needed some help. More than once a few of my buddies made sure I got home okay. I know Johnny Wilson took care of me a few times, and I hope he realizes how grateful I am for that.

When my family came to visit me at Riverview, they didn't know what my attitude was going to be. They didn't know if I was going to be angry, or depressed, or defiant. What they discovered was a man who was overwhelmed by the possibility of hope. That place was filled with great counselors and good people who were just like me, struggling to find their way back home. It's hard to say that I wanted to be there, but I understood that I needed to be there. That was an important step for an alcoholic.

I think the counselors understood that I was a candidate to make it the first time through. Two weeks into the three-week program I asked for permission to leave the facility to attend a signing session at a local card show. To be honest, we needed the money. They allowed me to leave, saying I would have to give a urine sample when I returned. Edna, Brenda and Dennis picked me up and took me there, and in that time away

from the center I had no desire to have a drink. I had
no desire not to return.

By then I think I knew I was going to make it
home. On the night before I left the center, I told Edna
it would make more sense for them to leave our car
there the night before, so she wouldn't have to come all
the way back to get me the next day.

I think my family members were concerned
about that plan, wondering whether I was going to stop
for a drink on my way home. I had been a closet
drinker, doing all of my drinking away from my family.

When I came through my door that morning
with a smile on my face, Edna said she knew I was going
to be all right.

I haven't had a drink since the night the family
confronted me. Has it been easy? Absolutely not. One
of the most challenging things for me was going to an
Alcoholics Anonymous meeting. The closest meeting
happened to be at my own church. I must have sat in
my car in the parking lot for 15 minutes, trying to
convince myself that I had to go in.

Not knowing who would be there, I was
concerned that there would be other members of my
church there. Certainly, I was embarrassed, but I went
in, and I kept going to those meetings in my church.

The members of the Detroit Red Wings alumni
association were all so encouraging. What you learn is
that you don't know who your friends are until you go
through situations like this.

Gordie and Colleen were among the first to call
and tell me how pleased they were that I had sought
help. You think you are fooling everyone, but everyone
knew I had a problem.

Once sober, I was able to restore my friendship

with John Curran. Ironically, many of our friends had blamed John for letting me go, saying he should have tried to help me instead. That was definitely pointing the finger at the wrong man because John Curran couldn't have been more generous than he was with the Gadsby family. When I left the Red Wings, Curran paid me more than the Red Wings were paying me to coach. I was making $25,000 and Curran gave me $25,000 plus bonuses. In the better years, the bonuses were $5,000 to $7,000. As a wedding gift to our daughters, he let them honeymoon at his home in Ocean Reef.

He passed away last year, but he knew how much I appreciated all that he had done for me and my family.

It's funny that once I got sober I started to see clearly how problems could develop. When we were in social settings, I could tell who the drinkers were. I would stand next to Edna, and say, "Listen how loud he is talking. An hour ago he wasn't talking that loud." I could see their mannerisms and their drinking patterns and know who was in trouble because that had been me just months before.

The AA program was difficult for me because I couldn't remain anonymous. Too many people knew my name, or me. When I entered a meeting, you could see and hear people whispering, "That's Bill Gadsby. He used to play for the Red Wings."

After a year of going to meetings, I decided that I didn't need them anymore, but I still wanted to do my part to help others. Dr. Finley has referred some hockey players to me to talk to, and I've done what I can. I don't know if it helped, but I told them the truth about what drinking does to your life.

Hopefully my story will help other families find the courage to deal with their loved ones who are overcome by this disease. The fact that my family would do this wasn't surprising to me.

These are the same daughters who came to me after we lost our savings on Autometrics and said they would all be willing to help us out financially if we needed. I didn't have to take their money, but their willingness to offer says a lot about how much we care for each other. My kids would do that for each other as well. We are all very close.

The reason I believe this intervention worked is that we all had a history together of a better time when I made it clear that my family was as important to me as life itself.

We had stories that we shared as a family, like the time we rescued a family of kittens from a dump by our cottage and named them Timmy, Tam and Tot. We called them the Dump Family.

In the 1950s, when Brenda was four or five, one of her schoolyard friends had told her that her dad was famous.

She thought famous was a bad word, and had argued relentlessly that her father wasn't famous, he was a nice man.

In my heart, I know that the love she had for me that day was the same love she had on the day she and her sisters sat in front of me telling me that I had to change to save my life.

Hopefully, my family all understands how grateful I am for their willingness to put themselves in an uncomfortable situation to bring me back. The one man I can't pass my thanks along to today is Dennis. He died of cancer a few years ago. He was only 48.

When he died, the memorial service at our church was packed, filled with some of those who worked under him in the construction business. Many had traveled three hours by car from a job site in Mt. Pleasant to pay tribute to this passionate man. He was a man who loved his family as much as I love mine.

He was such a passionate man that I believe he meant it when he said that he was going to physically drag me to counseling if that was what was necessary to get me help.

The year before he was diagnosed he and I went deep-sea fishing in the Atlantic, off the coast of Miami. Hopefully, on that trip he understood how much I appreciated him and how much he meant to me.

Despite the tragic loss of Dennis, I feel my life has been blessed since that day in October, 1988. Edna and I enjoy an incredible life together.

Edna has embraced the Alanon message, not just as a way to deal with alcoholics, but as a way to deal with life.

In January, 1992, she wrote in her journal. " I would have called Bill's alcoholism the saddest thing of my life, if not for the fact that because of this condition we have gotten to know God better. We are sent trials not to impair us, but to improve us."

Tears welled in Edna's eyes as she read that to us for inclusion in this book. From the moment I met her, I understood that she had a spiritual side and an intuition about life that would help me discover a better life.

My favorite story about non-drinking involves being pulled over by a police officer as I was leaving the Birmingham Country club a few years back. It turns out he stopped me because he thought I was driving suspiciously slow. That day I was driving slow because it was a residential area and I was just trying to drive safely. "Have you been drinking?" he asked me. "Not in many years," I said. He looked suspiciously at my cup holder. "You don't mind showing me that drink do you?" he asked. Never in my entire life was I ever so happy to show someone a cup of coffee.

Chapter 11

When I was playing in the NHL, it was important to me that Edna and my daughters not feel like they were second string in my life. To be honest, it can be difficult to balance a family life with a professional sports career. Nights away from home are difficult for loved ones you leave behind. People who travel for work understand. You leave to do your job and your spouse is left home to deal with small children. I never worried about my family because Edna was probably even better at her job than I was at mine. While I was playing for NHL All-Star teams, she was the real superstar of our family. I always tried to make sure that no Gadsby child or Edna ever felt like they were shortchanged because their father or husband was a hockey player.

When I started this book my goal was simply to be honest about the events of my life. In keeping with that spirit, I asked my daughters to write their thoughts on what it was like growing up as the daughter of a NHL play. Here are their words:

Brenda

Most of us don't remember the headlines we might have created yesterday. Applause dies. Trophies tarnish. Achievements are forgotten. Accolades and certificates may as well be buried with their owners. What really matters is the people who made a big difference in our lives. They may not be the ones with the most money, credentials or awards. They are always the ones who care. They are always the ones who matter. Their awards are in our hearts. I've had such people in my life. Friends and family have helped through difficult times. I've known special people who have shared their time with me; my sisters, a teacher, my friends and of course my parents.

When some fans recall my father, they remember the ultra competitor. They remember that he didn't hesitate a moment to drop in front of a Rocket Richard slap shot. They remember how skilled he was on the ice. They remember how tough he was in the corner.

When I think of my father, I think what a gentle man he was. I remember how patient Daddy was teaching me how to cut the lawn at our cottage in Wabamun. I remember how much fun we had creating that beautiful rock garden! We all loved Daddy's success on the ice, and loved being around the arena. We were all so proud when Daddy would come out of the dressing room and sign autographs. But when his girls get together we talk about how many times we drove Mom's Chevy convertible down to the store to get more gas for our boat. No man has ever had more patience for allowing his children to have fun than my father. He taught us to fish and to water ski. Some fathers will spend precious minutes with their children.

Daddy spent precious hours upon hours with his girls. There were trips up the glaciers in Jasper and Banff, Alberta, or family driving trips from the United States to Canada. I'm never going to forget my horse Beaujolais, or my surprise 16th birthday party.

To become a Hockey Hall of Fame defenseman, my father had to be devoted to his game, but he was also as devoted to his family as any father who has ever walked this earth.

I haven't, and should have, told my daddy what a great role model he has been or how his example has helped shape my life.

I haven't, and I should have, told my daddy how his courage in tough times has been my strength through the years.

Even though I may not always say what I really feel inside, I want the world to know how very proud I am to have a father as great as mine. The years have passed and his children are all adults with children of their own, and yet he's still the dad who makes everything more fun. We are all so lucky he is in our lives.

The best compliment I can give my father is just to say that he is the first man I ever fell in love with.

Judy Anne

When you hear about the children of famous athletes, you too frequently hear that the athlete was never there for his children. Our dad was always there for us.

This was a man who put as much energy into his children as he did into his Hall of Fame. In fact, he clearly put more into it because still today he is an All-

Star dad.

When the four of us get together and reminisce about growing up as the children of Bill Gadsby, we don't seem to recall how many days he was gone at training camp or at road games. We do remember all the times we spent together. That's certainly evidence that he did it right.

My dad had a reputation for tough play. He was always in the middle of the roughness. What do you think all of his opponents would have thought if they knew that he always let his girls put curlers in his hair for good luck?

On game days, Dad would always have his big meal early and then take a pre-game nap. I vividly remember jumping onto the bed and kissing him for good luck. And I remember fastening curlers to his hair for added luck.

The advantage of my dad playing 20 seasons in the NHL is that I can actually remember seeing him play. When Dad would come out of the dressing room after a game, I remember yelling "Hi Dad" just so the fans would know that was my father. When he was finished signing autographs, I would put my arm through his arm and walk with him. It was a proud feeling.

To be honest, I don't remember many bad moments being the daughter of a NHL star, unless you count the time when I was 15 and had a crush on a boy and I thought he liked me too. The reality, I soon learned, was that he just wanted to meet my father.

What we all remember was that being Bill Gadsby's daughter was a fun-filled adventure. When I was born, my dad played for the New York Rangers and we lived in Edmonton. I spent half of my time in

American schools and half my time in Canadian schools. The trips back home always seemed like a vacation because Dad would always travel 500 miles so he and his girls could spend a night in a hotel and go swimming. Dad taught every one of us how to swim.

One year we bought a new boat in New York and hauled that boat 3,000 miles back to Edmonton. We were all so proud of that boat.

We still laugh about the time that I got to drive home alone with Dad because Brenda was already in school. Dad said the only way I could go was if Mom cut my hair short so he wouldn't have to comb it and put it in a ponytail. Of course I didn't want my hair cut. I hated my hair short, but I got to be with my Dad. It was a reasonable trade as far as I was concerned.

When I think of growing up, I think of our summer days at our cottage in Wabamun. In the summer, Dad belonged to his children. You could tell he was as proud to be a father as he was to be a NHL player. What we probably understand now even more than we did then was that he would do anything for his girls.

One day Dad pulled me skiing 17 miles, the entire length of the lake, and then managed to drop me in the middle of a weed patch. I started screaming and the next thing I knew Dad was in the water rescuing me. Dad made us a homemade kneeboard, and when I was just learning to use it, I took a ghastly spill and sliced my knee open. Again Dad was there to rescue me. Dad was always there for us.

Dad always make it fun for us. We would vacation with Gordie Howe and his family, and sometimes we would go deep-sea fishing in Florida. (It wasn't fun if you got seasick. That's the only time Dad didn't have any sympathy for you. We laugh about that now.)

To be honest, nothing has changed between my father and me. Our relationship has the same warmth it had when I was a child. My Dad still calls me Doo-Doo, which he called me when I was a child.

We all know what a great hockey player he was, but to us he is just a great dad. My proudest moment seeing Dad in action came when he walked me down the aisle at my wedding 27 years ago. I will cherish that moment forever.

Donna

When we were young Mom told us never to brag about Dad, so maybe we should make up for it now. He is a hands-on dad who clearly had no regrets about not having any sons. He treated his girls, I'm sure, the same way he would have treated a son.

As tough as Dad was on the ice, he was never the disciplinarian at home. He just had a difficult time getting mad at his girls. He would always tell Mom that he would not punish us for something we did while he was away. That was probably unfair to my mother, but that offers a glimpse into Dad's personality.

He just wanted to teach us things, especially up at our cottage, which we owned for 21 years. He taught me how to paint, and we painted fences every summer. We built a huge rock garden. He tried to teach me how to golf, but eventually gave up.

Even today friends envy the relationship I have with my dad. This man who played so tough in the NHL tell me he loves me every time he sees me. We talk all the time. He brings me lunch when I'm working, and when I was working in an office he would bring me flowers on my birthday, which is the day before his birthday.

It's funny how life comes full circle. Now I have three boys, age 14, 18 and 20 and my mom and dad like to visit us at our cottage. Dad is always out with our kids, golfing or boating. He always has time for his children. When we visit them, the boys know that grandma will be cooking and grandpa will be talking to them. He likes to know what's going on in their lives. He cares.

When Mom wouldn't let us brag about our father, the way we would defy her edict was at the games at Olympia Stadium. We would always yell "Hi Daddy" very loudly so everyone within a six square block area would know Bill Gadsby was our father. I'm proud that many of my high school friends still call me Gads, just like my Dad's buddies called him.

Probably most people who just know me believe that I simply have a special bond with my father. That's simply not true. Dad is the same way with all of his girls.

Sandy

My father, who wore No. 4 throughout his career, has always believed that was his lucky number. Maybe that's why I have known so much pleasure as the fourth daughter of No. 4.

When I was born, my dad supposedly told the doctor that he guessed this means "I'm going to have to buy toilet paper wholesale."

For all the difficulty that is supposed to come with being the child of a professional athlete, all I have is wondrous memories of being the youngest member of our hockey family. My dad was a Hall of Fame defenseman on the ice, and he and my mother were Hall of Fame parents.

My dad loved to joke around with his girls. When I was just three, my parents bought a cottage on Lake Wabamun in Alberta and that place was always filled with joy and laughter. Dad called all of us girls his "little rag muffins". If we misbehaved, he would threaten to sell us to a Hobema Indian tribe that lived across Wabamun. We certainly didn't believe him.

This was a dad who never, and I mean never, said no to taking his daughters skiing. Even when it was raining we skied. The only time we couldn't ski was during visible lightning. In those years our speedboat probably burned more gasoline than the Queen Mary.

My memory bank is filled with visions of my father and I fishing at the point of the lake. When I was young I believed I was the luckiest angler in the world because every time my dad asked me to hold his rod so he could stretch or rest his arm, I would catch a fish. It was years before I figured out that he only decided to take a break when he knew a fish was already on his line and his daughter could get the thrill of reeling in the catch.

The summers at our cottage, near Edmonton, Alberta, were better than any amusement park you could go to today. Looking back, even work seemed like fun. I remember working on the bunkhouse with Uncle Ray Goss and that seemed like fun. (Maybe it was because I fell in love with every single Goss boy. It was a different one every year.)

My most memorable moment though, was right before we were moving to Detroit. We had a cat named

Bootsie and her daughter named Buttons who had six kittens and we had a very short time to find a home for them. My dad came home from the dump one day with yet another kitten in his pocket. When he was throwing the garbage over the dump, this little stranded kitten brushed up against his ankle and scared the living daylights right out of him because he thought it was a snake. He picked it up and brought it home. "Well," my mom said. "Bill, there has got to be more." So we all hopped into the wagon, with the fake wood on the side, and went back to the dump and found two more kittens. We then had 11 cats to find a home for in one week. Dad ended up taking them to a farm where we kept our horse, and Tim, Tam and Tot from the dump family, lived happily every after! Poor dad, that's the last thing he wanted to deal with before we made the big move to the Motor City. All of us were bawling because we had to leave all the cats behind.

At the age of five or six I was always at Olympia arena for the Red Wings Sunday practice. Every Sunday we would pick up two other Detroit defensemen, Gary Bergman and Doug Barkley. Those two guys taught me how to wink, and every time I saw them after that, even when I was an adult, I winked at them.

Just before Gary passed away I ran into him at the Joe Louis Alumni, and I gave him a wink. We always had a special bond.

The Olympia was my playground. Trainer Lefty Wilson used to give all the kids Juicy Fruit gum. I would meet Gordie Howe's daughter, Cathy, at the arena and we would run around the mezzanine and get into all kinds of mischief. We would raid the suites and drink soft drinks and devour snacks.

By the time Dad became coach of the Red Wings, I was already in junior high school. By then, I understood and appreciated the benefits of being an athlete's daughter.

We spent a lot of time with the Howe family and Mrs. Howe would spoil me rotten.

Detroit Red Wings owner, Bruce Norris, owned a place in Homasassa Springs, and we would go there every year. We got to do a lot of special things, like meet Gentle Ben (the bear), Clarence, the cross-eyed Lion and Judy the Chimp. We used to tease my sister, Judy, that she looked just like Judy the Chimp.

I also have a very funny story about Christmas involving my dad when he was coaching the Red Wings. It also involved my Grandma Gadsby, who would come to visit us from Calgary every year during Christmas. She was an awesome Grandma. I don't remember Grandpa Gadsby because he passed away when I was only one year old. Anyway, it was getting close to Christmas and we had not gotten our Christmas tree yet and Dad was catching a plane to go on a long road trip. So Dad and I went out to pick out our tree. When we returned, he put the tree in the stand and it was very crooked. He took the tree out in the garage and cut the trunk with the saw. When he put it back in the stand, it was still crooked. He repeated this process several times until the tree was shorter than I was! I started crying and said, "The tree looks horrible and it's shorter than I am."

Grandma Gadsby was sitting on the couch quietly and was watching all this time. My grandma never said a word. My dad never said a word, he just opened up the sliding doors, picked up the tree in the stand and threw it out the open door. It almost landed

in the neighbor's back yard. He was so mad and
stressed out, he almost missed his flight at the airport.
We have laughed about that for years. That tree stayed
out there until the spring thaw. Needless to say when
dad came back from the road trip, we went out and
bought a new tree with a straight trunk! Dad always
had to make it right for his girls.

I also remember the day my dad was fired from
his coaching job. Bruce Norris asked my dad to come
early to the game that night. We went to almost every
hockey game, but this particular night I went with my
older sister, Brenda, to her babysitting job. We were
listening to the game over the radio when we heard that
Sid Able was behind the bench and not Dad. Later we
found out he was fired for no apparent reason. That
may have been the only day it was difficult being Bill
Gadsby's daughter. The next day in junior high, some
bullies/brats started teasing me about my dad getting
fired. I just ignored them.

I soon understood that my dad had a lot of
friends and supporters in Detroit. We still continued to
go to the hockey games because Dad was scouting for
them, and we would hear fans chanting "WE WANT
GADSBY...WE WANT GADSBY." Everybody in the
whole Olympia would be chanting this. There was one
guy who made this huge sign that lit up with light bulbs
all the way around it that said WE WANT GADSBY
and walked around the circle of the rink.

It was cool to have so much fan support. We
believed our dad was the greatest and apparently the
Red Wings fans did as well. I would like to thank that
guy with the sign! I wonder how the owner, Bruce
Norris and general manager, Sid Able, felt that night?

Much later, when my dad played for the Detroit

Old-timers, I went to most all the games. We would take a bus and after each game there would always be a gathering. We would have to wait for my dad after the game and he would be one of the last players out of the locker room. Only later did we find out that they would drink a lot of beer!

I never knew my dad swore until one night when he was skating to the bench and I heard a string of cuss words. I couldn't believe my ears. He never swore in front of his girls, and when he heard our boyfriends swear at our house, he kicked them right off the property. He would literally toss them into their car and tell them never to come back.

I have too many memories to have a favorite. I do remember when I was growing up I was a good softball player and a cheerleader. My dad was never too busy to play catch with me in the backyard, and he was at every game to cheer me on.

My mom and dad mean everything to me. I am thankful for our days together. I'm also a grateful Gadsby.

The Book Team!
Aaron Howard, Del Reddy, Marty Reddy, Mike Reddy,
Steve Grauss-DC Sports, Bill Gadsby and
Mr. Hockey® Gordie Howe
Not Pictured
Writer-Kevin Allen and
Felix Gatt-Creative Impressions, Inc.

**A special thank you to a remarkable
lady, Edna, for her diligence and hard
work during the prepartion of this
book.**

A Message From The Publisher

Mike Reddy

The publication of "The Grateful Gadsby" is the first book for Immortal Investments L.L.C. We are proud that this remarkable story commemorates the launch of the publishing division of the company.

Gadsby's inspiring story merits immortalization. It is our hope that readers who invest their money and their time will be rewarded with books that move, inspire and spotlight the best of the human spirit.

This publishing venture is also unique in that the book will not be sold in book stores. It will only be offered directly through Immortal Investments Publishing, appearances by Bill Gadsby, through the web site or by ordering online at www.billgadsby.com or www.immortalinvestments.com

You may also call us at 1-800-475-2066 to order your autographed copy today!

Immortal Investments Publishing
A Division of Immortal Investments L.L.C.
35122 W. Michigan Ave.
Wayne, Michigan 48184